"I'M NEVER DRINKING AGAIN"

"I'M NEVER DRINKING AGAIN"

HOW TO STOP DRINKING SO MUCH & CHANGE
YOUR RELATIONSHIP WITH ALCOHOL

DOMINIC MCGREGOR

CAPSTONE
A Wiley Brand

Registered Offices

John Wiley & Sons, Inc., 111 River Street, Hoboken, NJ 07030, USA

John Wiley & Sons Ltd, The Atrium, Southern Gate, Chichester, West Sussex, PO19 8SQ, UK

For details of our global editorial offices, customer services, and more information about Wiley products visit us at www.wiley.com.

Wiley also publishes its books in a variety of electronic formats and by print-on-demand. Some content that appears in standard print versions of this book may not be available in other formats.

Library of Congress Cataloging-in-Publication Data is Available:

ISBN 9781394232802 (Paperback)
ISBN 9781394232819 (ePub)
ISBN 9781394232826 (ePDF)

Cover design & concept by Nick Entwistle & @OneMinuteBriefs

Set in 11/16pt and Adobe Jenson Pro by Straive, Chennai, India.

SKY10072497_041224

To every person who's managed to make a positive change in their lives. Any positive change, no matter how small, can open the door to a world of possibilities.

I didn't believe I'd make 7 days, but here I am 7 years later.

Thank you to everyone who has supported me on this journey.

To my wife, Georgie, thank you for everything.

To my mum, Louise, you are the reason I am who I am, thank you.

To my Dad, Brian, thank you for giving me your work ethic and determination to better myself.

CONTENTS

PREFACE

On 24 July 2016, I made a decision in my life to go sober. This wasn't a decision I wanted to make, it was a decision I had to make. I had founded a company at the age of 19 with Steve Bartlett now of *Dragon's Den* and *The Diary of a CEO*. We were working with the likes of Disney, Spotify, and Microsoft and we were one of the fastest growing, most exciting companies in the United Kingdom. I couldn't handle the pressure, so I decided to drink to numb the pain that this was creating in me.

After months of managing to hide my alcohol dependency, I ran into a number of problems, all self-created, which meant I almost lost everything: the business, my friends, my family, my partner (now wife) – everything I spent my life working for. Like Icarus who flew too close to the sun, I was a 23 year old who had played with fire too much and was left with no option but to make a change in my life. So at 23 years old, after an intense period of therapy, I tried going sober. The first few thoughts that entered my mind after making this decision were centred on how my life was going to look without being able to drink or go out. Up to this point, I had experienced life and alcohol through a very narrow lens. This felt like a huge change, and I was uncertain about how it would work.

At the date of publication, I am 30 years old and 7 years sober. I have now officially spent more time in recovery than

I was ever legally allowed to drink. In that time, I have managed to take my company to the public markets – listing it on the German Stock Exchange – as well as start my second business, host a TEDx talk, win countless awards, invest in over 20 companies and marry my best friend. Removing alcohol from my life has allowed me to reach my full potential and grow into a person whose life is rich with friends and meaningful relationships, and who has hope for the future.

While alcohol has become a social norm in much of the Western world, and many people believe they have a healthy relationship with it, it is still an addictive drug. What is insidious about it is that when life is good and stress is low, you are able to enjoy it "carefree". During those times, when the hangovers don't take days to get over, when the anxiety in the morning is manageable, when your body bounces back, it's all okay. No one in those situations would admit that their relationship with alcohol is negative. But our relationship with any addictive substance is deeply rooted and can swiftly change when circumstances around you do.

I am fortunate to have gone through what I did at 23 years old. The strain of running a business with over 100 people at that young age artificially increased my dependency on alcohol and effectively fast-tracked me into having serious issues. My issues with alcohol happened at 23, however, without addressing the underlying issues around my relationship with alcohol, these issues could have happened at 33 or 43, as I never questioned my relationship with alcohol *until* it became a problem. This book is for everyone, *everyone* who can enjoy a drink – to help you understand any current or future warning signs. It's for everyone waking up with a hangover on a Sunday morning and thinking to themselves "I'm never drinking again."

There is a shared experience for many who have gone "sober": most people have a rock bottom that acts as their wake-up call, and I was no different.

What I learnt when I hit my rock bottom was that the answer for me was sobriety. It was the only option I had. Not everyone is like me, there are others who can manage this relationship better. My relationship with alcohol, however, was so bad that it had to end. I have experience in staying in relationships too long and I end up doing significant damage to myself. If you're anything like me, think to yourself: Do I have a healthy relationship with alcohol? Do I have a healthy relationship with stress and anxiety? Is my mental health okay? What do I do in those situations when I don't feel well? Do I reach for the glass of wine too quickly?

The debate around alcohol has shifted in the past 7 years, the time I've been sober. At 23 years old I told my friends that I was "Never Drinking Again" and they looked at me as if I had just insulted their entire family with some senseless joke. It was a statement no one believed, partly because of who I was, but also because it was very rare. Seven years later I've been exposed to the sober community, which is full of wonderful men and women from all over the world and from so many backgrounds. I have never felt so welcomed.

Now at 30 years old, I am frequently told by peers, strangers on the internet and those closest to me that they "wished" they could stop drinking, but it's become too ingrained within their life. I have also experienced firsthand the damage alcohol can do to families and relationships, having been a drunken disgrace previously. I now witness that with people close to me, who don't know when enough is enough. This has led me to write this book, sharing some of my experiences, the experiences of others in the sober world, and my learnings from going from someone who had a stable, loving upbringing by an incredible Mum and Dad alongside a solid private school education to a 20-year-old Jack-the-lad to a 30-year-old sober husband. It's my heartfelt wish that my experience and tough lessons learned will help anyone who might need to change their relationship with alcohol too.

ACKNOWLEDGMENTS

To my family:

Georgina McSorley, Louise McGregor, Brian McGregor, Henry McGregor, Oliver McGregor, Matthew McGregor, Louise Dunn, Judy McSorley, Jim McSorley, Shaun McSorley, Laura McSorley, David Hobbs, Lydia Walter, Margaret Hyde, Janet McGregor, James Hyde, John McGregor and Philip Hyde.

To my friends:

Steven Bartlett, Ashley Jones, Anthony Logan, Oliver Yonchev, Michael Heaven, Sam Bamber, Toby Joynson, Chris Brooksbank, Nik Gunson, James Aubrey, Sam Fox, Joe Rodgers, Josh Harland, Jacob Hields, Adam Johnson, Charlie Yates, David Newns, Rachel McDonald, Emily Smithies, Hattie Gibson, Whitney Mellor Adams, Lisa Sayers, Jamie Dempsay, Sophie Chapman, Georg Kofler, Christian Grobel, Holger Hansen, Wanja Oberhof, Sean Brown, Jack Brewitt, Richard Johnson, Hannah Anderson, Jess Brindle, Cathal Berragan, Jay Mottershead, Andy Ramage, Ruari Fairbiarns, Matt Pink, Catharine Gray, Millie Gooch, Stephane Elswood, Patrick Kennedy, Jack Law, Paul Stevens, Ansar Mahmood, Steve Oliver, Jeremy Roberts, Chris Donnelley, Dave Lucas, James Cox, Carla Speight, Claudia Cardianli, Megan Stolz, Oliva Bushell, Ross Methven, Taby Martin, Ali Scott, Jonathan Coe, Jake McCormick, Charlie Hirst and Harry Hope.

ABOUT THE AUTHOR

Dominic McGregor is a 30-year-old entrepreneur and mental health and sobriety advocate. Dominic is currently a Founding Partner of investment fund Fearless Adventures and ex-COO of the global marketing agency, Social Chain.

Along with his co-founder and fellow university drop out, Steven Bartlett, Dominic helped grow Social Chain to a US$300 million turnover business with 750 staff in offices around the world, including New York City, Berlin, and London.

After building a global client portfolio that includes the likes of Apple, Amazon, McDonald's, and the BBC, the pair took the company public in 2019 and then exited in late 2020.

Post-exit, Dominic co-founded Fearless Adventures, a company which invests in founders who are looking to rapidly scale their business. Through this venture, Dominic passionately uses his experiences and huge wealth of knowledge from building and scaling a successful business to nurture new talent and support other entrepreneurs on their journeys both financially and emotionally.

In early 2021, Dominic was appointed by the Cabinet Office as a government policy advisor looking at social media and digital communications.

More recently Dominic and the Fearless team have created Basecamp Academy, with a mission to nurture, coach, and up skill in all things digital, creating industry leading talent. The Basecamp co-founders believe that businesses need cultural and professional diversity to succeed, and they are helping to provide life-changing opportunities and enable the business community to build teams with different perspectives.

In 2023, Dominic became a feature in the BAFTA nominated and award-winning documentary series *Hollyoaks In Real Life*. His episode 'Alcohol Free At 23' saw him talking to *Hollyoaks'* long-standing cast member James Sutton about his journey with alcohol addiction. He also talks candidly about the pressures of running a successful global corporation, the expectations within that Wolf of Wall Street environment and how he felt during his journey to sobriety along with the changes he has seen since.

Alongside all his business and career successes, Dominic has found time to become a public speaker at a variety of events, including the likes of Capital One, Microsoft and many more, along with featuring in globally recognised news publications. He brings forward topics such as mental wellbeing, tech and digital skills, business strategies and success, and more besides, utilising his own journey through a variety of bespoke keynotes, opinion pieces, feature interviews, commentary, and panels to inspire and educate audiences of all sizes.

CHAPTER 1

TOP OF THE SLOPE

I'll never forget the day when I felt like I had completed life. It was 26 September 2015. I had just flown into New York to attend the UN's Global Goal festival, which Beyonce, Ed Sheeran and Coldplay were headlining.

I had been invited by a major Venture Capitalist Investor who had invested early in the music platform Spotify. This was the world 22-year-old me was living in.

A world of investors, business class flights, top hotels and amazing food. This was probably the fourth time I had been to New York that year. We were considering opening up an office in the United States for our company, so the trip had a real purpose behind it. This was going to be our third office location and in time, hopefully our biggest.

I had fallen in love with New York when I first saw it as a 19 year old. There was a special feeling about seeing the lights in Times Square at 4.00 am after flying down Fifth Avenue drunk in the back of a yellow taxi cab, which I believed were just from the movies until I travelled to the United States. The next few times I visited I began to fall in love with Central Park and other areas of the city more occupied by locals than tourists. At 22, I felt a strange feeling of belonging, being comfortable in New York, knowing my way around and starting to feel like it was home.

So, on 26 September, here I stood, at the top of my slope, unaware of what the months ahead held. As the day started, I woke up in the city that doesn't sleep after a glorious business-class flight into New York. I was staying in a 5-star hotel just off Central Park. My business partner Steve and I had been invited to the Global Citizen Concert and we were in the VIP section; because the concert was in Central Park there was no alcohol allowed in the regular areas. I think if I'd had a normal invite, I would have politely declined – the ability to drink and party was a major pull. We arrived at 12.00, walking past the Strawberry Fields – the tribute to Beatle John Lennon, a nice little reminder of the power that music has to move people.

Ultimately, we were out of place here – two young British entrepreneurs in New York at this global event. The speakers included Leonardo DiCaprio and Michelle Obama, and it was hosted by Hugh Jackman and Olivia Wilde. This was the day of days. It felt like everyone who was anyone would be at this event. They'd be in the VIP section, and more than likely at some point we'd see them. So we infiltrated the bar and began to give ourselves a bit of "Dutch courage".

It was here that I started seeing people I recognised. I caught sight of a beautiful woman with long ginger hair – I was sure I knew her and I was pretty sure she was British, but I couldn't place her. Google didn't let me down – Bingo!

Bonnie Wright who played Ginny Weasley in the *Harry Potter* movies.

Slightly star struck, I took a bit more Dutch courage to navigate the occasion. Bonnie Wright was a big name, but she was far from the only one. Turning around to see Jaden Smith and the (real life) Winklevoss twins (who inspired my entrepreneurial journey in the movie *Social Network*) really blew my mind. The alcohol flowed to give me the confidence to be around these people. I felt like an imposter. My mind was racing . . . *What am I doing here with these people? I'm just a young guy from York – this doesn't happen to other 22-year-olds. This is wild.*

I knocked back another drink to quieten the thoughts running around in my head. The day continued with talks from major world players. We watched Coldplay open the show from the VIP section, which was literally 10 yards away from the stage. Behind me 60,000 New Yorkers were thoroughly enjoying their day, despite being unable to get a drink. While at the bar, I looked at the TV and noticed Leonardo DiCaprio on stage giving his speech – I hadn't realised he would be here.

I turned to Steve in disbelief and asked, "Is that here, is this live?" He said, "I think so." Something came over me and I said, "I'm going to find him."

I had an irrational determination to find Leonardo DiCaprio. I had no idea how I'd do that. I had no idea what I'd do when I did, but I became fixated with this quest.

So I set off.

During the show, I'd seen a small gate with two rather large security guards. By now, I was well "on my way" and my drunken conclusion was that there was probably a VVIP area or Green Room where the performers and speakers would be. This gate seemed to me like the logical target – if I could infiltrate it, I might find Leo. I knew my time was limited, it wouldn't be long until he was off stage and more than likely heading somewhere else (people like him do not hang around for long). I made a beeline for the gate, approaching the security guards with the utmost confidence, covering my wristband with my sleeves so they wouldn't see what category of guest I was. I walked up, head held high, and without being asked a single question, walked past them and into the other behind-stage location.

Steve followed me. Part of me felt like we had done it, we had made it. As we stepped into the backstage area, Leonardo DiCaprio was coming off stage – surrounded by security guards. Noel Gallagher right in front of me. I came within touching distance of Leonardo, manoeuvred between his security guards, reached out my hand and . . . stroked his arm.

What a crazy guy I was – who did I think I was, stroking Leonardo DiCaprio? He didn't even really seem to notice. I was buzzing. The day continued and the alcohol continued to flow. We partied with huge A-listers like Jay Z, Kanye West and Chris Rock, but the highlight for me was following the prime minister of Japan into his Green Room. It was a total blag. As he came off stage, I joined his security guard, who were all Japanese, dressed in suits, and holding shoulders to form a human shield. In my purple jumper and jeans I didn't think I'd get away with it, but I joined the back of the train and when a guard asked, "Are you with them?" I confidently said, "Yes".

Now, what I learnt was not only was the security terrible, but that drinking gave me a deluded confidence. I was probably close to committing a few felonies or at least breaking some international law that day, but not for a second did I think about that. I was just thinking, *this is the life; this is what you're supposed to be doing at 22 when you've built this business.*

Little did I know then that this was far from what I was "supposed" to be doing. Before this I was always a drinker, always someone who would have fun. I remember the end of year awards, when your school year voted for 'The most likely to do *x* and *y*'. We had the usual categories: most likely to be on Spotify, most likely to write a book (which I would have probably been bottom of), and most likely to be a spy – the usual trivial things that 18 year olds go for. The award that I proudly won – 'Most likely to be drunk right now'. That was me, a Lad. In the intervening four years, little had changed. On 26 September 2015 aged 22 I reached the peak of my alcoholic adventures. From that day on, every day slowly unravelled in my life and the journey to rock bottom, to a place of nothing but pure personal torture, had begun.

ASCENDING THE SLOPE

Being a VIP at a high-profile event in New York was a very long way from my first home – Old York. After the house parties and turning 18, I managed to scramble my way to university to study Sport Science – not that I knew what I wanted to do 'when I grew up' but I knew for sure that I'd love to work in sports. I had always loved sports and when choosing a course to study I thought about the old saying, "If you do something you're passionate about you'll never work a day in your life." This was probably the main bit of life advice I wanted to follow. I believe I went to university well rounded. University is the first time a lot of people have the freedom and opportunity to live their lives. Away from the watching eyes of parents, many people begin to find themselves and experiment. From my point of view, I had already done a lot of that while in my late teens. I would say that I was an early drinker.

My first alcoholic drink was at my Dad's 40th birthday party. At that party there were WKD alcopops, which were the craze at the time – the ones that looked like fruit juice. I was 13, a month away from my 14th birthday, and way below the legal drinking age, but being surrounded by my older cousins who were at the time 16, 17, and 18 years old, I was able to steal a taste of my first drink.

You might think there's nothing unusual in that, but the age at which you begin consuming alcoholic drinks is more important than you probably realise. Studies[1] show people who begin drinking before age 15 are four times more likely to become alcohol dependent at some time during their life, compared with those who have their first drink at age 21 or older. There I was, unaware that I had increased my chances of becoming addicted by 400%, just for a bright blue drink and a bit of fun at a family party.

University saw me proudly continue this trend. I was a great, fun drunk – there have been many nights of serious fun. The nights you reminisce about with your friends when you get together. Days when you're strolling home with a pizza and hearing the birds start to sing, but you know it isn't an issue because tomorrow you do not have a lecture until 3.00 pm. On those days, you genuinely know you can sleep in till 2.00 pm and even then missing that lecture isn't the end of the world.

University is fun – at least it was for me. You take yourself out of your comfort zone, to a new city. Little me from York could pack his bags and move 200 miles to Edinburgh, get away from parents' watching eyes and their judgement and start to live the life I wanted to. The life I wanted included the achievement of taking Fleetwood Town to the Premier League title on FIFA 12 by 2023, well over 24 hours of gameplay. Sorry to all the Shrimpers out there, but now in 2023 Fleetwood are no closer to the Premier League title than they were back in 2013.

Those 10 years have flown by. But the good old days do quickly disappear and so does our ability to bounce back from the hangovers and hangxiety of the mornings after. I'm comfortable yet somewhat crazy, maybe, to admit that I never felt anxious, depressed or really in touch with my emotions at university or school. This has been a common trait amongst my male peers – we don't talk to people, we bottle things up and we don't tend to show emotion. As a young male, this can be very damaging as it means we are unable to process and therefore handle things around us. Growing up is always difficult and as we transition from childhood to adulthood we have a lot to learn. All of this development is overseen by our brains.

ISSUES WITH ALCOHOL

Our brains don't fully develop until we're around 25.[2] This applies regardless of gender. However, there is also research to suggest that the process of reorganising connections in our brains (which is what leads to maturity) begins earlier in women than in men.[3] The simple truth is that adult and teenage brains function differently. While adults engage their prefrontal cortex – the brain's rational centre – during thinking processes, teenagers do not possess the same level of development in this area. When viewed from the perspective of neuroscience, it's easy to see the hazards of alcohol consumption among anyone under the age of 25.

When we take this alongside the fact that female brains tend to develop earlier than male ones, it offers a potential explanation as to why it's often boys we remember doing stupid things at school. As puberty starts, female brains jump to at least 2 years older than their physical age. Males, however, usually take until their late teen years or even early 20s to match their female peer's mental age.[4] With a more mature brain than men, women tend to have a stronger sense of responsibility sooner than men.

Throughout the stages of adolescence and early adulthood, the brain undergoes a series of transformations, establishing neural connections, trimming unused pathways, and refining regions accountable for functions such as decision making, impulse control, and strategic planning.

These transformative processes intricately contribute to the cognitive and emotional growth of an individual.

This means that when we're under 25, certain cognitive functions linked to mature decision making, risk assessment and impulse control aren't functioning at what is considered an adult level. This has consequences for behaviours like alcohol and substance use, propensity for risk-taking, and overall decision making. We're treated as adults at 18, but for many of us our brains have another 7 years of development ahead of them.

Throwing alcohol into the mix alongside an undeveloped brain explains why so many 'nights out' tend to include young men fighting in the streets or jumping off bridges. It explains why men tend to be the ones doing stupid stuff while drunk. One study among 15- and 16-year-old students in Ireland found that 19% of young men admitted to being in a fight when drunk, 17% have been injured, and 23% have lost property. The statistics do not lie – drinking leads to problems.[5]

Despite this, the world seems to love alcohol, there is a cult-like protection around alcohol that other toxics and drugs do not experience. For example, I have never been questioned about why I do not smoke. We are all aware of the danger of smoking (which is legal) – yet people chose to do it. No one questions someone else's right to choose not to smoke – and no one walks around sticking a cigarette in your mouth saying "get it down you". No one panics around Tesco looking for a present to buy their friends on their 21st and rushes to the cigarette aisle to buy them a 20 pack. No one says to people during a hard week at work, "You need to smoke an entire pack of fags, that'll make you forget all the shit you've been through."

I hope most of you are like me and think that the idea of the above sounds a bit icky . . . a bit socially unacceptable and grotesque.

There was a time, when cigarettes were glorified, where claims were made that they were healthy for you. Back in the 1950s and 1960s advertising very often pushed health claims about cigarettes. One such example was Marshall's Cubeb[6] cigarettes claiming to be a "sure remedy" for asthma, nasal congestion, and the common cold. I often question whether the world is that different today given that we're now told instead that vaping is healthier than smoking.

Alcohol is currently on the same trajectory as smoking – there is a widely accepted belief that alcohol is not good for you. In the United Kingdom in 2019 alone there were 358,000 admittances into hospitals where the main reason was attributed to alcohol.[7] That is one admittance every 1 minute and 30 seconds due to alcohol.

Alcohol-related harm is estimated to cost the NHS in England £3.5 billion every year.[8] This does not factor in the long-term side effects of drinking. Chronic alcohol consumption can lead to liver diseases such as fatty liver, alcoholic hepatitis, cirrhosis, and liver cancer. Prolonged alcohol use can impair cognitive function, memory, and concentration. It may also increase the risk of developing neurological disorders such as Wernicke–Korsakoff syndrome. What's more, chronic alcohol consumption can weaken the immune system, making the body more susceptible to infections.

Yet, still we toast with champagne to celebrate or down a pint to commiserate.

In a world where we are starting to believe that health is our wealth and are seeing the rise of healthy eating, holidays in which we spend more time exercising than lounging around the pool, the short-term and long-term side effects of alcohol are staring us in the face. Whenever I meet someone and explain to them why I do not drink, I realise that it is not yet universally accepted that some people choose not to drink – and that we have very good reasons to do so.

Suppose I sit you down and seriously talk to you about a choice you can make in your life. It's a very straightforward one, where some of the upsides include the following:

1. Physical health: Abstaining from alcohol can lead to better overall physical health, including improved liver function, reduced risk of heart diseases, better sleep, and maintaining a healthy weight.
2. Mental clarity: Not drinking alcohol can help maintain clear cognitive function, sharper memory, and improved focus.
3. Emotional well-being: Avoiding alcohol can contribute to better emotional stability and mental health, reducing the risk of anxiety and depression.
4. Productivity: Abstaining can lead to increased productivity, better work performance, and the ability to pursue hobbies and interests with more dedication.
5. Improved sleep: Choosing not to drink can lead to better quality sleep, which has numerous health benefits.

And, to complete this, it actually saves you money... If you shared all of those benefits without mentioning alcohol, most people would be dying to know what they needed to do to obtain all these benefits. However, when you tell them "Well, it's simple: just stop drinking alcohol," many people straight away refuse the deal.

If I could develop this as a product (like a pill or gummy), I would become incredibly successful and rich, because these are areas in which people strive for improvement constantly.

Having said that, the United Kingdom appears to be waking up to the benefits of stopping drinking, at least for a finite period of time. In 2021, an estimated 6.5 million people in the United Kingdom were reported to have participated in Dry January.[9] Though come 1 February (or even 28 January) our lips start to shiver and we crave the sweet nectar of booze. We once again begin the cycle that results in either Friday, Saturday or both nights drinking and heading to nightclubs to either "socialise", to avoid *Ant & Dec's Saturday Night Takeaway*, or to take the stress of the week away. As is true for most, I've been told by friends, "You just need to blow off a bit of steam, just have a drink." Or "It will be okay, just have a glass of wine." Or "That calls for a glass of fizz to celebrate." Our emotional tie with alcohol is deep.

Eighty-four percent of men say they want to drink less, yet the global consumption average is 6.2 litres of alcohol per year. That works out as 53 bottles of wine per person per year – a bottle a week. Although males still outpace females for most alcohol-related measures, the gaps are narrowing, For cohorts born around 1990, males outnumbered females roughly 3:1 for measures of alcohol consumption (e.g., prevalence, frequency) and problematic drinking (e.g., binge drinking, early-onset drinking). Many of these ratios are closer to 1:1 today.[10]

The reason I've shared these statistics with you is to demonstrate that, certainly in Western societies, we have deep-rooted issues with alcohol, and that even where our drinking habits might not be considered problematic or damaging in a societal context, damage can and does happen under the radar. It took me to hit rock bottom, very hard, to recognise my issues with alcohol. I want to help you spot yours long before you have to fall that far.

WHY ME?

This book isn't going to give you a high-horse opinion from someone who doesn't drink – it will give you insights into how a young man, unable to manage his emotions, stress, and strain turned to alcohol as a coping mechanism to get through a difficult period. As the difficult period continued, the drinking got worse and worse – so much so that drinking itself became the problem. I like to think about myself as incredibly average, just a normal guy who loves football, time with friends and family – you've probably met someone like me 10 times over and will see my traits in your peers after reading this. What I discovered can happen to anyone, as the wheel of life turns. We all need to develop outlets, to manage our stress – but I've learnt that alcohol isn't a healthy outlet and while one drink every now and again is never an issue, there's always a path on which that one drink could lead to a few more.

My real downhill spiral began when I felt I reached a peak in my life. I unknowingly pushed off the top of my slope on 26 September 2015, as I stood in Central Park surrounded by celebrities and VIPs, glass of champagne in hand. My descent lasted until the last day I drank on 23 July 2016. Over these 9 months, my life imploded. This is an incredibly short space of time – so even if right now you are living your best day, and your best life, and believe me, I was there – you are within a few small changes from hitting your rock bottom. On the way down you'll hurt yourself and others and what I've learnt is that alcohol – on many of these occasions – can be the ingredient that gives the slope its slip.

One of the things that started my "slip" was the feeling of being an imposter and the decision to give myself some "Dutch courage" to get me through.

DUTCH COURAGE

While there is no consensus over where this term came from, one of the most popular theories links it to the Anglo–Dutch Wars that took place in the 17th century. During these conflicts, English soldiers and sailors observed that their Dutch counterparts would often consume alcohol before battle to calm their nerves and boost their confidence. The English supposedly began using the term "Dutch courage" to describe this phenomenon.

I've had countless conversations with friends and have advised others to "have a bit of Dutch courage" when facing social anxiety.

Social anxiety is the worry about not fitting in, in a social setting. It's that feeling of going to an event, like a wedding, and chucking a few drinks down you to lubricate the conversation, to avoid the self-doubt of "what am I going to talk about with them?", or "what if people think I am boring?" – all little comments and worries we tell ourselves.

I've seen Dutch courage used when dating, maybe when meeting a person from Tinder who you want to impress so you have a drink to bring your personality out and make yourself a bit more entertaining.

Is there any logic or science behind this?

Alcohol can affect the brain, reducing inhibitions and creating a feeling of confidence or fearlessness. This feeling can lead people to take risks or face situations they might otherwise avoid. For example, one study suggested people were more likely to have the courage to interact with people they considered attractive after a drink[11]. I certainly had my share of Dutch courage at that event in New York. As I said, I felt like an imposter and this was my way of coping in that situation. Of course, none of us really need alcohol though, even when we feel it will help.

WHY DO WE DRINK ALCOHOL?

After going sober, often the first question people asked me was "Why don't you drink?" At first I answered by explaining how it negatively impacted me and caused me a number of personal challenges with my life.

For many years I was happy with that answer, as I felt that, yes, I was the black sheep going against the grain – so many continue to drink even when they should stop. Then one day, at an event, I was feeling slightly tired and in one of those moods where small talk was going to be an effort. I asked politely for a non-alcoholic drink – my options were either Coca Cola or water – and on asking this, one of the individuals in our conversation said to me, "Just a quick question: why don't you drink?"

Out of a mixture of frustration with the lack of non-alcoholic options combined with being slightly tired that day, I responded with:

"Why do you drink?"

From the look of confusion I saw, it was obvious this was the first time the woman in front of me had been asked this question. As she held her champagne flute she looked down into it, took a sip of it and responded, "I don't know, because I like it."

Over the past few years, I have continued asking, "Why do you drink?" to anyone who asks me "Why don't you drink?" There've been a number of times when it's obvious from the tone of the question that I am the anomaly, that I am the one doing something unforgivable. Over the past few years I have not been given a response to my question that I would class as a reasonable explanation as to why someone drinks. It has long been a question I've wanted to answer though – why, really, do we drink?

To address this question, I want to look at why an individual wouldn't go sober.

There have been a number of studies in this space. One in particular by the charity Drinkaware found that 60% of young people (18–34 year olds) in the United Kingdom cite social pressure as a reason to drink. The study suggests peer pressure is ingrained within our culture, with many people associating drinking with being sociable and seeing those who don't drink as boring or outsiders.[12]

Dr Emma Catterall, Evidence and Research Associate at Drinkaware said: "The danger is that if people interpret peer pressure, or encouragement to drink, as part and parcel of convivial drinking culture, it could become seen as acceptable behaviour. The reality is that peer pressure to drink, in whatever form, encourages people to drink more than they might intend."

So, 60% of young people are drinking so they are not perceived as "boring" or "different". Young people are unconsciously forcing each other to drink, but also to drink more than they intend to. Encouraging people to do more of something like running, working out or working hard isn't an issue – but alcohol is an addictive substance.

Would you be surprised to read that alcohol is the most frequently used addictive substance in the United States? In the United States 17.6 million people (or 1 in 12) struggle with alcohol. Like many, the image of an addict I had when I was younger was one of someone who literally cannot function, is skinny and potentially hair is falling out. This was such a naive opinion – and an inaccurate one. It wasn't long before I was introduced to the world of high-functioning addicts, people who frequently consume too much alcohol, cocaine or other substances and turn up the next day at 9.00 am for work like nothing had ever happened.

Why did I drink?

This is a question which I have pondered over for the past 7 years, why did I succumb to alcohol dependency?

My views on it now are pretty defined.

The Conversation identifies the following four types of drinkers:[13]

1. Social drinkers

Social drinking is likely perceived as helping you have more fun with your friends. According to research into what motivates teens and young adults to drink alcohol, social motives are the most commonly cited. This aligns with the idea that drinking is a social activity. Those who drink primarily for social motives typically consume moderate amounts of alcohol.

2. Those who drink to conform

People who drink to fit in on social occasions rather than because they would normally drink alcohol, tend to drink less than those who drink for other reasons. These people will often nurse a drink to avoid feeling different from those drinking around them – perhaps they'll have a champagne for a toast or hold a glass of wine to avoid being put under pressure to drink.

As The Conversation noted, programmes like *Hello Sunday Morning* have been encouraging people to take a break from drinking in recent years. By making not drinking more socially acceptable, such programmes may be decreasing the negative reactions some people experience when they choose not to drink.

3. Those who drink for enhancement

This is one of the riskier reasons to drink that has been noted among adolescents and young adults. Those who drink for enhancement are more likely to be extroverted, impulsive and aggressive, according to the article in The Conversation. They are also more likely to have a risk-taking personality and to drink alcohol because they want to feel drunk.

4. Those who drink to cope

Finally, The Conversation identified a fourth group – those who drink to cope – noting that these individuals tend to have low self-esteem and higher levels of neuroticism than others. People who fall into this group use alcohol to "cope" with problems in their lives, including those related to anxiety and depression.

The fourth group also tend to consume more alcohol and experience more problems related to alcohol than those who drink for any other reason. Although this might feel like a valid tactic in the short term, it leads to serious negative consequences in the long term, often because the factors that led to drinking as a coping mechanism are not being examined or addressed.

I started out as number 1 and slowly, without realising, moved to number 4.

I did believe though, at some point in my life, be it my late 40s, early 60s or mid 20s, that I was going to have a problem with an addictive substance. Like many people, I believed I had an 'addictive personality'. There have been studies into whether addictive personality exists. *Psychology Today* says,[14] "The reason is because addiction depends, first and foremost, upon having an addictive personality. Such people, estimated at perhaps 10%–15% of the population, simply don't know when to stop."

However, addiction to any substance is not quite so simple as whether you have an 'addictive personality'. An article on the American Addiction Centers' webpage[15] explains that the idea of someone having a generically 'addictive personality' is a myth and instead offers evidence for the fact that while there is no one personality type that leads to addiction, there are certain traits that can put you at a higher risk of developing an addiction. The organisation goes on to share some seemingly disparate traits that can lead different people to become addicted to drugs or alcohol, depending on other factors like socioeconomic status or, as mentioned previously, the age at which you first drink.

When my alcohol consumption was moderate and enjoyable – during my early teens – there was no sense of addiction. Alcohol acted as the natural social lubricant as it does for so many people and it enhanced my life and in parts made it more enjoyable and fun.

So, why did I fall into a downward spiral?

The main reason was due to my relationship with alcohol and 'why' I drank. Even from a young age when I was playing sports, alcohol was seen as a celebration and a kind of mood manager. We have probably all heard of the saying "win or lose – we're on the booze". This saying comes from UK culture and it means whether the outcome is good or bad we are getting drunk.

I remember vividly thinking this prior to my A-levels. I was either going to celebrate or commiserate.

I remember after football matches having a good pint to either drown the sorrows of defeat or celebrate a victory.

I remember my own birthday parties as an excuse to get ridiculously drunk and celebrate with my friends.

I remember getting dumped by a girl and getting so drunk that I wouldn't remember it even happening.

I remember my grandad passing away and 6 hours later being so crazy drunk that I was rolling under a parked car (which I thought was funny at the time).

I remember feeling confident and excited for a night out and thinking *I'd love a drink right now.*

While all these examples may seem pretty insignificant and very normal for people to read and experience, this behaviour began to build an emotional relationship between my mood (or mental health) and my alcohol consumption.

While small fluctuations in anyone's mood are very common, regulating them with alcohol is not a good or healthy approach. I had never really had experience of the problems and challenges that life throws at you as you grow and take on more responsibilities, so I was ill-equipped to deal with them when they arose as I approached my 20s.

The reason I said so confidently that I would have had the problem in my 40s or 60s is because I never learned a healthier way to manage my emotional variance. This is a common issue with men – this is what bottling up your emotions can do to you. It leads you to look at different ways to communicate how you are feeling and how to express your emotion.

I didn't have an addictive personality and, similar to the articles just referenced, I don't believe that those exist. Addiction isn't something that targets a specific segment of our community who may be biologically different, or have a certain predisposition – it doesn't discriminate, it's something that everyone has the potential to fall into if a couple of things in their life fall a certain way. There may be an element of genetic impact, but this is far from the whole story.

I have spoken with Prof Steven Peters, author of the book *The Chimp Paradox*, about alcohol. Prof Peters argues that the logical pre-frontal cortex of the brain is who we really are – it represents the human within us. The more emotive limbic system, on the other hand, operates more primitvely and he calls that part the 'chimp brain'. The 'chimp brain' can be more powerful than the 'human brain' given the right triggers and stimuli.

Recent research has shown that addiction can also be 'built in' to our brains. Genetically loaded. The gene in the brain kicks in around the mid-20s. If you have this gene, you're more likely to be unable to recognise when you should stop drinking alcohol. This gene is seen within 1 in 8 people. Like many, you would go out with the intention of "only having one drink" but if you have this gene, you will find it much harder to stop there. Maybe this was me. But 1 in 8 people in our world is 1 billion people; 1 billion people are at risk of not being able to only have one drink.

Often this switch in drinking habits will occur following some kind of trigger. For example, the removal of a safety net, or being catapulted into a situation that you are unable to handle – such as humongous amounts of pressure – can launch you into addiction. Major personal trauma is another trigger point, which can lead someone to begin a downhill spiral and find themselves using alcohol to manage their emotions, to forget the pain that has been caused and to escape reality.

That was also part of my journey.

It could have happened later in life, but it happened to me at 22.

What causes someone, in the space of a few weeks, to go from living their best life in New York, to entering a downhill spiral and systematically destroying their life?

MY TRIGGER POINT

The trigger for my downhill spiral happened on Friday 13 November 2015.

This was supposed to be one of the best days of my life. Over the past 6 months, we had been working on raising another round of investment. We had grown the business to roughly 30 people and begun to get a great amount of momentum and recognition within the industry.

To give you some brief backstory, Steve and I created our business while we were students and, ironically enough, it all started with a Tweet about a lack of toilet paper in my bathroom. The inspiration for this Tweet came after a night of drinking. I woke up, went to the bathroom and realised we were out of toilet paper in my student house. The next decision I made changed my life: I set up a Twitter account and posted a Tweet about it. I called my page Student Problems. I would talk about all the things I was "discovering" as a student – like how expensive cheese is.

Within the first couple of months I'd amassed 20,000 followers and had started to create memes. Managing social media became something of a side hustle for me. Then I met Steve, Social Chain was born and everything escalated very quickly from there.

We were the "kids who were controlling what other kids spoke about".[16] This quote comes from an article that accelerated our growth. For those who want to get a bit geeky and understand just how fast the company was growing, our annual growth rate (CAGR) for the 3-year period went from £250,000 in 2014 to targeting £4,500,000 in 2016. You can use the following formula to calculate this rate of growth:

$$CAGR = (\text{Ending Value} / \text{Beginning Value})^{\wedge} (1 / \text{Number of Years}) - 1$$

So let's calculate the CAGR:

CAGR = (4,500,000 / 250,000) ^ (1/3) − 1[CE2]
CAGR = 18 − 1
CAGR = 17

The CAGR for the 3-year period is 17, or 1700% (expressed as a percentage).

We were on track to grow 1700% − as two young kids only 22 years old at this point!

On Friday 13 November 2015, our investment money came in. All £1,000,000 of it! You might be wondering why, if everything was going so well, this date was when I started sliding down that slippery slope. Let me put this into context to help you understand the pressure Steve and I had been under, for quite a prolonged period of time.

I had dropped out of university almost 2 years earlier, after realising that being "lectured to" wasn't for me. I had lost my initial energy for my studies and found myself drifting towards only scraping by in the second year of my course. I knew university wasn't right for me, and I had ambitions to do something else. Steve and I had set up the business and it was doing well, I made the leap.

It wasn't long before the business was flying. When we were offered £1,000,000 in investment to continue to grow the company we were excited. However, we were also in need of the money. We had made a few major errors while running the business – firstly, with payroll. We had hired an accountant called Jane to do our bookkeeping and payroll. We thought this was a smart idea, so that at the end of every month we'd have a breakdown of how much money the whole team was owed.

On payday, we paid them.

This went on every month like clockwork. The last Friday of every month was payday and we never missed one.

However, we hadn't realised that we had to do more than just pay our staff. One day, my assistant Lisa came to my desk and said, "HMRC are here."

God, what the hell?! My mind went into a panic, this is the taxman – the dreaded taxman.

Feeling terrified, I watched as an unassuming man in a suit walked into the office and sat opposite Lisa and I. He told us that we owed almost £100,000 in PAYE, which we hadn't paid. We were both shook to our cores. £100,000 – at the time that was pretty much all the money in the bank account.

I rang Steve, feeling like we had no option but to pay it. Given that this was the taxman, we did.

No one, not Jane, had told us that after paying wages you have to pay HMRC. This was just an oversight by two young founders who were trying to grow a business. Remember that we were only in our early 20s. Off the back of this, we also found out that Jane was not actually doing our accounting at all – we discovered no work had been done on our 'books' since we started trading.

This cost us a lot of time, energy, and mental space to revisit 12 months of trading.

The lesson I learnt here and that I give back to founders every day is the importance of financial literacy. Numbers may not be the most enjoyable part of running a business but having a strong understanding of them is going to save you getting tripped up down the line.

But the HMRC debacle wasn't our only challenge. Since August 2015 we had been involved in a legal investigation with the Competition and Marketing Authority (CMA). They were working to investigate the rise in social media marketing and whether 'ads' were being clearly displayed as such.

This investigation required us to hand over all our contracts, proposals, invoices and emails that we had in the business with any clients or influencers since 2014. This was a major project for which we had to pull in a specialist barrister at a major cost – we felt we had little choice as the potential fines could have been all our revenue, if we had been seen to mislead any client.

This investigation was ongoing in November 2015 – but we felt confident that we hadn't broken any legislation. In fact, off the back of this investigation with the CMA, the gold standard of #AD became the way people recognised an advert on social media.

Challenge number three came from our rapid success and lack of financial understanding. Our cashflow was growing as we began to work with clients like Disney, 20th Century Fox, and Amazon. The contract values grew larger and larger. In fact from our first year where our average campaign was between £5,000 and £10,000, we were now frequently billing over six figures per project.

What nobody told us was that these big players had standardised 60–90 day payment terms. We were operating on roughly a 50% margin including staff costs. This meant that winning £500,000 of work in 1 month would mean we'd have to pay over £250,000 out before we saw a penny of that.

Our rapid growth led to major cash flow problems which we, at 22 years old, didn't have the experience to manage or maintain. As part of the investment we were going to bring in a chief financial officer (CFO) who would be supporting us in this area.

Finally, all in the space of a few months another major challenge presented itself. A few days before we agreed to the investment, we were victims of a cyber-attack.

I had woken up. It was a normal day and Steve and I, who were living together, drove into work separately.

My phone rang and Steve asked, "Why did you send that email?" I felt perplexed. We'd been together literally all morning and I hadn't sent an email. We each pulled over at the side of the road.

I logged into my emails. Between 4.00 am and 8.00 am that morning someone had accessed my account and sent malicious emails, pretending to be me, to our entire client base and our potential investors.

As 8:30 am struck, replies began to come in. Some of our biggest clients pulled their entire budget, the investors told us they were going to reconsider their position.

Our intention for the day had been to go paintballing with the team as a way to celebrate all the incredible work. That went out of the window in a heartbeat. We met everyone at the office and swiftly sent them all home. Steve and I stayed in the office, this needed to be solved and fixed. From 8.30 am to 9.00 pm we did all we could to salvage what we could. There was a point during that day in which I thought everything had gone. We had lost. But we persevered.

We managed to rescue some, but not all, the clients and the question marks from the investors remained. To this day, I do not know definitively who did this to us. I probably never will. Do I still think about it? Yes.

So, in a few short months we had been landed with a huge HMRC bill, were involved in a legal investigation, had run into cash flow issues and were victims of a cyber attack.

Of all of these challenges, you might think that the cyber attack would be the one I'd be the most angry about. But actually all I can say is "thank you". I'm thankful for the lessons this taught me. I'm thankful because this cyber attack, which caused the worst day of my life at the time, started the build up to what would become a tidal wave of problems that all came crashing down on me. And although it might sound odd to read this at this stage of my story, I'm thankful because this negative event, and the ones I'll share that followed, made me a better and happier person.

This is the backdrop to that fateful Friday 13 November. That morning, the first thing I did was check the bank account. It was like Christmas. The investment had landed and I was looking at a bank account with over £1,000,000 in it. I ran downstairs to tell Steve and it felt incredible. It felt like all our problems were over and that we had achieved a major milestone in our business.

It was time to celebrate! I was taking my girlfriend at the time to Paris. As you can imagine, over the past few months work had been a major priority to me and this was a chance for me to spend some quality time with her and unwind after all the stress. At the airport we got a glass of champagne and were on our way.

I had decided I wanted to treat myself and with football being a major passion of mine, I'd bought us tickets to see France vs Germany at the Stade de France. As soon as we landed, we headed to the stadium. Unknowingly, we were walking into the heart of a terrorist attack. Our plane landed slightly late, so we were on a mission to make the kick off. We were 5 minutes late for the game, so we snuck into the stadium. As we walked to our seats we heard this loud bang. Looking behind us we saw security and police running out – we didn't think much of this at the time – but as we were desperately late we took our seats to watch the game.

Germany were up 0-1 at halftime. They had the game under control and as it was only a friendly match, we decided to leave before the final whistle. Our plan was to escape early and beat the crowds so we could get back to our hotel room but when trying to leave the stadium, we realised we couldn't leave through the normal exit. This is when things started to seem wrong.

Our phones were almost dead after a long day of travelling so we set off back into Paris blind. Before our phones died, we managed to catch up with the news. A bombardment of messages flooded in, asking if we were okay. All we could gather was that there had been explosions and shootings – and that the situation was ongoing. While we got the basics of the information, like most, no one really knew what was going on.

We were lucky to leave the stadium early – the majority of the fans trying to leave after us were held in the stadium for their safety. We spent the next hour walking in fear down the streets in Paris trying to find our hotel. Every taxi was taken, and we were terrified turning every corner. All we knew was that there was still a situation going on, we just didn't know where or how close we were to the violence.

This was when I experienced my first major panic attack. My heart rate increased, I felt out of control, and I began to break down and become laser focused on survival. There were some specific moments that still trigger me to this day. At one point while going down an avenue in Paris, 19 police vans drove past in a line, sirens blaring. When that happened, we swiftly turned around – we had no idea what we were facing, but we sensed it was highly dangerous.

On that night, 130 people were killed in the French capital in a series of shootings and bombings, including 89 who died in the deadly attack on the Bataclan concert hall.[17] While we didn't know the details of the situation while we were trying to navigate our way to our hotel, we were hyper aware that this was not only not normal, but that we could be in very real danger.

When we managed to make it back to our hotel, my first thought was 'I need a drink' so I poured a glass of red wine and tried to calm myself. The trauma was suppressed with drink, I never really dealt with these feelings and chose to drink, once again to forget. This was the trigger for my slide down the slope to my rock bottom – months of stress followed by a day that started with elation and ended with terror. You might think it's understandable that I turned to alcohol that evening. But understandable or not, I can say with certainty that it didn't help me.

NOTES

1. National Institute on Alcohol Abuse and Alcoholism (1998). Age of drinking onset predicts future alcohol abuse and dependence. https://www.niaaa.nih .gov/news-events/news-releases/age-drinking-onset-predicts-future-alcohol-abuse-and-dependence
2. Gloom. (2015, February 19). *At what age is the brain fully developed?* MentalHealthDaily. https://mental healthdaily.com/2015/02/18/at-what-age-is-the-brain-fully-developed/

3. Newcastle University (2013). Brain connections may explain why girls mature faster. Science Daily. https://www.sciencedaily.com/releases/2013/12/131219131153.html

4. Kayla Denker (2011). Girls' brains mature faster than boys': fact or fiction? The Hiller. https://thehillernewspaper.org/3846/hiller-hall-of-fame/girls-brains-mature-faster-than-boys-fact-or-fiction

5. O'Keeffe, C. (2020, June 4). One sixth of teens in fights after drinking. *Irish Examiner.* https://www.irishexaminer.com/news/arid-20422781.html

6. Sandee LaMotte (2017). The history of tobacco health claims. CNN Health. https://edition.cnn.com/2017/05/24/health/gallery/tobacco-health-claims-history/index.html

7. Digital, N. (2020, February 4). *Around 360,000 admissions to hospital as a result of alcohol in 2018/19 - NHS Digital.* NHS Digital. https://digital.nhs.uk/news/2020/around-360000-admissions-to-hospital-as-a-result-of-alcohol-in-2018-19

8. England, N. (2019, January 5). *NHS England » NHS Long Term Plan will help problem drinkers and smokers.* https://www.england.nhs.uk/2019/01/nhs-long-term-plan-will-help-problem-drinkers-and-smokers/

9. UK, A. C. (2023, May 17). *Press release: 6.5 million people plan to do Dry January 2021, up from 3.9 million in 2020.* Alcohol Change UK. https://alcoholchange.org.uk/blog/press-release-6-5-million-people-plan-to-do-dry-january-2021-up-from-3-9-million-in-2020

10. Aaron M. White (2020). Gender differences in the epidemiology of alcohol use and related harms in the United States. Alcohol Research Current Reviews. https://arcr.niaaa.nih.gov/volume/40/2/gender-differences-epidemiology-alcohol-use-and-related-harms-united-states

11. Joe Pinkstone (2023). Why you can't put on 'beer goggles' – but you can pluck up Dutch courage. *The Telegraph.* https://www.telegraph.co.uk/news/2023/08/30/why-you-cant-put-on-beer-goggles-but-can-show-dutch-courage/#:~:text=But%20scientists%20have%20found%20that,to%20be%20a%20real%20thing

12. Drinkaware (2020). Peer pressure to drink is experienced among adults of all ages. https://www.drinkaware.co.uk/news/peer-pressure-to-drink-is-experienced-among-adults-of-all-ages

13. Emmanuel Kuntsche and Sarah Callinan (2018). There are four types of drinker – which one are you? The Conversation. https://theconversation.com/there-are-four-types-of-drinker-which-one-are-you-89377

14. Stephen Mason (2009). The addictive personality: If drugs are addictive, how come I'm not addicted? *Psychology Today.* https://www.psychologytoday.com/us/blog/look-it-way/200903/the-addictive-personality

15. Marissa Crane (2023). What are the traits of an addictive personality? American Addiction Centers. https://americanaddictioncenters.org/the-addiction-cycle/traits-of-an-addictive-personality

16. Luke Baily (2015). Meet the company secretly running all your favourite social media accounts. Buzz-Feed News. https://www.buzzfeed.com/lukebailey/the-social-chain

17. BBC News. (2015, December 9). Paris attacks: What happened on the night. *BBC News*. https://www.bbc.co.uk/news/world-europe-34818994

CHAPTER 2

GLASS BOTTOMS

"First you take a drink, then the drink takes a drink, then the drink takes you."

F Scott Fitzgerald

Unknowingly, I was beginning to become my own timebomb. By not dealing with issues, learning coping mechanisms, or maturing, I was setting myself up for a dramatic downturn. I had done nothing to prevent myself from falling into an addictive relationship with alcohol.

One of the things I never realised about running a business was the interest other people had in you. There was always someone who wanted to meet you. I didn't always see what they wanted. Sometimes they were genuinely curious to meet and discover what you've done. Sometimes they wanted to sell you something – often something you might not have needed, but sometimes it was something that might actually be useful. In addition to these meetings, I was also frequently invited to events.

Events in the industry are also interesting. People fall into a number of groups, but the mainstay of people who attend events are the religious networkers who believe that meeting as many people and kissing as many frogs as possible is the most impactful way to grow their business. As someone who was very anti-networking to begin with, I admit I changed my perspective somewhat and do see value in carefully selected events to build your network – that said, by networking too frequently you can become a busy fool and presence and attendance at events becomes your objective, reputation and identity as a business owner.

As a young founder of a relatively cool company, our event invitations included new restaurant and club openings across the United Kingdom and even in New York, Ibiza, and Dubai. These were too good to turn down in my early 20s, but I didn't know they would be my Achilles heel.

BROKEN ANKLES AND REGRETS

I remember fondly an invitation to the restaurant Neighbour-hood's reopening in Manchester. This was the place to be in 2015. Everyone who was anyone would come here – *Love Island* stars, footballers, entrepreneurs. As a team we spent New Year's Eve 2015 here spending thousands of pounds on bottles of champagne and vodka. In fact, this was what we did on a lot of our weekends while the business was scaling and having success. Our Friday after-work drinks would roll into Neighbourhood very quickly. The invitation to the res-taurant's reopening was limited to Steve and I as founders, but we were able to bring those close to us. At this point we began to separate founders from the rest of the team and we were starting to have our own independent lives.

This was not a night to miss. It was exclusive and a soft open on a Thursday before the official opening on the Friday. So, like most of the events I was lucky enough to go to, everything was free. This was a common pattern at any event. Free food and free drinks – what an easy way to assure you got a great attendance. This is the universal code for people who come to an event; the bribe that planners make to assure people have a good enough reason to come. At this point my mindset was such that I had begun to expect this from events and if this wasn't the case, I would decline.

The 'free drinks' lure always assumes an exclusive event for people you want to be seen at a venue or event, people who have clout on a local level, but also people who can afford the cost. We live in a society where money has long been the only currency people accept as payment, but with the growth of social media there has been a more in-demand currency, one which companies, brands and people are more willing to accept – clout. While I was going about my life on a daily basis and running the business, I never really considered myself as someone who would enter that category of becoming influential.

But others clearly saw me as someone of influence, hence why I was invited to the likes of the Neighbourhood reopening.

At this point on my journey, I had become famous for "disappearing" on nights out. It was just expected of me – so there was an acceptance amongst those around that nothing would be out of character if I wasn't there and, as I had proven a number of times previously, I would be able to get myself home safely.

With my friends thinking of me as something of a homing pigeon, I knew they wouldn't miss me or worry if I headed elsewhere. I was free to do what the beast inside me wanted to do. It was a dream situation for someone who is dependent on alcohol.

The Neighbourhood reopening could have just been a typical night out for someone who wasn't deep down struggling in silence, but in hindsight all the warning signs were there – it was an explosion waiting to happen.

The booze flowed freely and I took advantage. At some point, I must have left the venue. In true homing pigeon style, I made it home and woke up the next day in my own bed. It was 25 miles and a good 45-minute drive from the event (not that I drove home, I must have got a taxi), so this has to be seen as a success. You take those mini victories when you can find them. But that was the only victory that day.

Not only had I slept through three alarms, my phone was bombarded with missed calls and messages from people in the business. When I woke up, the time was close to 11.00 am. I knew I had a meeting with clients at the office, which there was no way I was going to make.

When you wake up after a night of heavy drinking, your memory and feeling comes back in pieces, and you are slightly numb in your body and mind for the first few seconds. This is known as confusional arousal – those first few seconds of waking up before everything comes flooding back to you. Entrepreneur Tom Bloomfield explained it best when talking about him running Monzo. He said "When I did sleep a full night and wake up at 7, 8, 9 am, for about 3 or 4 seconds I'd forgotten what my life was. I'd forgotten what I was doing, what my job was, all the pressures and I was calm. Not stressed, not anxious and then 3 or 4 seconds later all the memories came back and it was just like a crushing weight."

In my case after this night, while the familiar feelings begun to return – the headache from dehydration, the anxiety telling yourself you fucked up – there was a new feeling in the mix this morning. One of real pain and discomfort.

My knees were sore and my ankle was in tatters – it felt broken, it looked the size of a tennis ball and the colour was closer to purple than a skin tone. What had happened? In good time the memories started to roll back.

After getting dropped off by the taxi, I had slipped on our driveway. We lived at the top of a hill, which meant that, long into spring, we still had wintery conditions. In fact, that year the last bit of snow was on 1 May – I remember this as it was just a week before my birthday. Not only that, but our house was off this hill and had a steep drive down towards the door. We lived in a gated community of three houses, and taxi drivers were reluctant to drop us off at the bottom, so they would helpfully pull up at the top, as we'd have to get out to enter the code for the gate anyway. Therefore, to get back to the house, I always had to navigate the drive, which when sober or sensible was never an issue. But when I was in the state that I was in that night, it was a gamble. A gamble that I had lost. As my memory started to piece together what happened, I clearly remembered that, while navigating the icy drive, I had tripped over and twisted my ankle (albeit that morning I thought it was broken while lying in my bed).

At 3.00 am, lying on my driveway, I was paralytic (that is to say, extremely drunk and therefore struggling to coordinate any of my limbs. In short, I could barely walk). In fact, I was so paralytic that I couldn't get off the floor.

I was stuck, there was ice on the floor, it was slippery, I was drunk, my ankle was hurting. I was like a defeated tortoise on my back. I knew deep down that in a matter of hours I had got meetings with clients looking to work with us, not to mention a team of over 50 people at this point, some of whom were joining me in the meetings. And here I was, stuck on my icy driveway. At the time, my only thought was of getting into my bed, but the reality was I just wanted the pain to end, and the only way I could do that was by closing my eyes, going to sleep and letting my body start the recovery.

My aim was to get back to my room, which was 50 metres down the drive. I had to open the door, climb the flights of steps, and with any dignity I could muster, get into bed. The only option I had was to crawl, dragging myself inch by inch down the drive. (That explained the cuts on my knees.) So that was what I did. I crawled past my car – another reminder that in the morning I had somewhere I had to be – and when I got to the door, I manoeuvred myself to sit down and reach the handle. The one thankful piece of this journey was that we were irresponsible, so irresponsible in fact that we never locked our doors, so during this process I didn't need to stand and apply any pressure to my ankle. I continued to crawl through the door and then, stair by stair, I scaled the three storeys to my bedroom.

Now, if you looked at my life on social media at this point, you'd be thinking, doesn't this guy have everything? Isn't he living the dream? He's running his own successful company, always hiring for fun and creative roles, just bought a Rolex, is getting invited to exclusive parties of new places opening, getting to go back to his seven-bedroom, three-storey house with an attractive girlfriend in the suburbs and has a new Mercedes car.

The truth was I was very lonely and disconnected from everyone around me. The house Steve and I lived in was about 25 miles outside of the city. I'd physically removed myself from people. It meant I could never text a mate and ask if they just wanted to hang out for an hour. My decision to move myself to a beautiful house in the middle of nowhere was one of the worst things I could have done as someone who was on the borderline of struggling with an addiction.

I was isolated in more ways than one. My life was very different to that of other 22 year olds. Many of my peers couldn't relate to the kinds of problems we were facing in the business, nor could I imagine being in a world where my biggest problem was hitting my next uni deadline, or a boss I didn't like. I emotionally isolated myself from my friends, and instead of talking about my struggles, buried them further under a veneer of "living an amazing life".

That was the view I was portraying to the world, but at that moment when I got into bed a piece of me didn't want to ever wake up in the morning – because I knew the damage I had done to myself and to the company.

I chose to sleep through the alarms, knowing that staying in my bed and not waking to the reality that I was going to face would be a much better choice. The idea of eternal sleep was starting to appeal to me. I liked the thought that I'd never have to face repercussions for my actions. Closing my eyes to the world and not waking again seemed like a blessing.

You think this would have been the moment when I made the choice to turn away from drink. You might think that at this point I had had enough. This had been the accumulation of months of unknown and undiagnosed anxiety, imposter syndrome, insecurities – of my own destructive voices in my head telling me I do not deserve what I have; that I am going to lose it all; that I am a fraud and a failure; that I am not good enough. This is what I was trying to deal with – but at that point it wasn't yet the bottom.

This was a fake 'rock bottom', what I call a *glass bottom*.

BREAKING A GLASS BOTTOM

How do glass bottoms work? Well they work in the very same way to glass ceilings, except while breaking glass ceilings is positive, breaking glass bottoms is negative. You can break through a glass ceiling, it isn't a real ceiling – once you break through it, you enter a world of positivity and possibilities that you could have never imagined yourself reaching.

When you break a glass bottom, you enter into a world of despair; a world of new pains that you have never experienced. This is on the way down to a rock bottom. The rock bottom is the point where there is nowhere else you can go. It's a bottom, so deep, so solid and so alone that the only thing you can do as an individual is to start making steps to move forward and climb. The truth is that hitting a glass bottom does hurt, you'll get a few cuts on the way, but it doesn't break you. You break it.

On my journey, I had a few glass bottoms, a few moments I believed were so damaging that I was at the point where I was ready to make a change – a point where this was the wake-up call. The morning that I woke up after the Neighbourhood opening was one of those. The feeling I had when I knew I had to go to hospital and miss more of the working day to check if my ankle was okay was one of wanting to go back to sleep and forget this ever happened. I had hit the place where you want the world to swallow you back up and spit you out somewhere so far away that it doesn't matter anymore. But, you can't escape your reality, you can't escape the problems you create – you have to deal with them.

This happened on 2 June 2016. A whole 7 weeks before my final D-Day, before I hit rock bottom. This was my final glass bottom, the one that hurt the most. The troubling part about it was that I had started to become a master of lying. I was constantly lying my way out of the problems I created. Here I was on Friday, seeking sympathy from people in the office, my girlfriend at the time and from friends, family and clients. All of whom had little idea that this was self-inflicted; instead it was something we all laughed off as a stupid, drunken mistake. In fact, I remember people being overly sympathetic with me, and I used that to my advantage. At this point, I was in the downhill spiral, and the fall down my drive was myself releasing the brakes on my train-wreck of alcoholism.

I received no punishment for my actions that night – clients forgave me, colleagues hoped I was okay, my girlfriend rushed to help me. My evil thoughts were still present and I knew that alcohol quietened them. I had also reinforced the belief that my actions did not have serious consequences. This, as a belief for a 23 year old, is dangerous. You begin to believe you are better than others, that you are free, that you deserve better, that you can do whatever you please and no one is going to question you.

This was what I had learnt, indirectly, from 3 years of running my own business, raising over £2.5 m in invest-ment, and generating over £4 m in revenue. There were two people inside my mind. There was this anxious, scared little boy and there was the evolution of 'Drunk Dom' beginning to form – a rotten, cocky, obnoxious, arrogant young man. One of them was starting to win the battle for my body and soul. One of them fed on alcohol to bring out the worst in me. The other was far too scared to speak up and to take control of the mothership.

This was a ticking time bomb waiting for something else to go seriously wrong – Drunk Dom was no longer the fun, playful, adventurous drunk that people knew me for. I wasn't the Drunk Dom who had no problems. I had become a much more sinister version of Drunk Dom; one who was destructive and was now able to take full control once I had a drink.

At this point, I still hadn't acknowledged that my drink-ing was a serious problem. I still wanted to take advantage of the exclusive events and free booze that accompanied them. I wanted to ride the wave as a young business owner who was disrupting the world and society was supporting me with those ambitions. I'm not blaming others for my own shortcomings, this was a problem all of my making. But at this point, the way British society viewed entrepreneurs had changed, and that also accelerated my slide to the bottom.

GROWING UP IN THE DIGITAL AGE

In the early 2010s there was a wave of positivity towards entrepreneurs that hadn't happened before. Previously business owners were commonly middle-aged white men, who started a business after many years of success in an industry, or alternatively were nepo (nepotism) babies who had inherited their family businesses. It was a pretty exclusive club, with not much access to outsiders.

Tech changed this. In the United States we saw a number of huge success stories of significantly younger founders. I remember watching the movie *Social Network* for the first time – an 18-year-old at university in Edinburgh watching an 18-year-old at Harvard University getting his friends together to start what, at the time, was a website. But as we know, that website (Facebook) changed the world. The art of the possible had begun to be achieved by younger and younger people, and with technology, younger people had the advantage.

The iPhone was released when I was 16 years old, so I am old enough to know what life was like before we had the world in the palm of our hands, but I witnessed the dawn of the digital age as a child. I grew up with a landline in my house. When we got a modem (which used the landline) for internet connectivity, there was competition between using the phone to make a call or using the modem to be online; we couldn't do both at the same time. Next, I remember specifically the day we got our first 'wireless' phone. I asked my Mum, "Does this mean I can now take this to football training (which was literally 100 m down the road from my house) and then ring you when I have finished?" My Dad quickly interjected, "No, you can only make calls from the house with this."

Then as a 9-year-old, I remember holding a real "mobile phone" for the first time. In my teenage years I was fortunate to possess both the legendary Motorola Razor and the Sony Ericsson Walkman phones – both played a major role in the digital evolution. In 2004, the debate was about not "when" should a child have a mobile phone, but "if". This is different today, now it is a rite of passage and it's a given for teenagers, and even younger children, that at some point they will be given a phone. In fact they may have exposure to personal technology in the form of, for example, iPads much younger than I was when we got the internet, let alone when the mobile phone debate was happening.

I was thankful I was a second child because my parents had stepped back a little from their overly cautious approach they took with my brother Matthew. Because we were only two years apart in age we were very frequently treated equally. If he got a new toy, I'd get a new toy. This may have annoyed Matthew, as he had a longer wait. Myself, I'd simply walk in with the newest shiny thing – which I was slightly smug about. Of course this continued when it came to getting our first mobile phones.

Tech created a democratisation of opportunity in business, which saw younger, more dynamic entrepreneurs start to lead the way. This was especially true in the United Kingdom that was dominated by financial and more traditional industry. No one else could operate in a new field like social media better than young people who had lived the majority of their lives with these platforms available. As one of these younger entrepreneurs, disrupting the status quo, invites and curiosity frequently came my way. Hence why I was at Neighbourhood, getting so drunk I couldn't even walk down my own drive.

HIDING IN PLAIN SIGHT

Although the events I was attending might seem like the dream situation for someone else – weekly opportunities to eat, drink, and party at someone else's expense – they had a dramatic impact on me, someone who was struggling. As mentioned in Chapter 1, I was now on major unstable ground, but without knowing it. Dramatic life changing circumstances had happened over the previous 2 years and I couldn't handle the uncertainty and anxiety that had crept into my life. I was looking for a release as well as something, or someone, to blame it on.

There's no easier way to cover up a drinking problem than maximising free drinks. Let me explain why.

Anyone struggling with any form of addiction knows that the addiction hurts them emotionally, mentally, but also financially. Someone with a betting addiction is always going to chase their losses – if you give them free money to play with, the bets will be bigger and the high of getting money back without any risk will be higher.

As someone struggling with drinking, an open bar is the home run, the holy grail of circumstances. Knowing in the morning there will be no financial repercussions for my actions, it's an easy "get out of jail free card". Also, no one can count up how many I've had – there is no better feeling than that.

Being able to walk into the bar feeling totally comfortable that the beast inside me is going to be able to feed, drink, and get away with it . . . what could go wrong?

As someone looking to drink as much as I could, I can't stress enough how freeing it is knowing that no one will be able to count your drinks. When going on casual socials around others, it is very common to get into "rounds", where among a group you each buy one another drinks. This is a social phenomenon that actually regulates how much you drink because it gives power to someone else in "the round" to determine when you can next drink. Additionally, at a cash bar, you have queues blocking you; so at a busy place you can be moderated by delays caused by having people in front of you. As with all addictions, your desire to have more needs feeding as quickly and as often as possible and socially we've managed to slightly limit that when it comes to alcohol. Finally, you have friends around you who could call you out – saying things like, "why does he keep disappearing?" or "slow down, that's like your fifth drink".

That said, when you're out with a small group it's easier to sneak in extra drinks. Having just a small group limits the eyeballs on you. It may be easier to stand out when there are four of you, but it's also much easier to get away with grabbing an extra drink here and there.

So, a small group (as I said, it was only Steve and our partners who were invited to the Neighbourhood reopening) plus a free bar was a home run for Drunk Dom. When I look back now, I can see it was an accident waiting to happen.

CHAPTER 3

FILLING THE VOID

Alcohol leads to broken promises and shattered trust – the building blocks of any relationship.

At this stage of my life Drunk Dom was only out to do one thing – screw up Sober Dom's life. Alcoholism is a selfish disease, at this point not only had I become a master of lying, but I was also hiding bottles of wine all over the house to drink when needed, and not mixing friendship groups so as to prevent anyone from spotting trends. Having four big weekends every month with four different groups of people never felt wrong – to them it was one big weekend a month – which can be classed as "normal".

Alcoholics are masters of self-destruction. When anything that starts going positively for them, as soon as alcohol is introduced, their drunk version somehow manages to "f**k it up". You turn off potential suitors, there's a negative impact on work professionalism, and a souring of relationships through your actions, the list can go on. This feedback loop leads you to be more desperate, lonely, and needy. All of which, for someone who is using alcohol to regulate their moods, means that you end up drinking even more.

This was my cycle – inside I was vulnerable, lonely, and scared, so instead of acknowledging those emotions and acting on them, I chose to drown them out with a bottle of wine. That wine led to the creation of Drunk Dom, a version of me who is the opposite to who I really am. Drunk Dom is angry, shortsighted and brash. Once he started entering delicate areas of Sober Dom's life, there was only going to be one outcome.

SELF-DESTRUCTION

At the time there was a list of things I had started to hold dear to myself. These included, in no particular order, the business, my family, my girlfriend, and my friends. Unfortunately my drunk actions had alienated a few of these people. One in particular of these I will not forget – this is perhaps an open apology.

I chose a path different from others. I chose to drop out of university to pursue a deluded dream with little chance of success, a huge chance of failure, limited security but a good chance of learning along the way. Many others made more noble choices of going into careers like medicine, choosing to put others before themselves and pursue a career in helping others. One such person in my life, my longtime friend Rebecca, chose the honourable path and sought to become a doctor, a route no sane person would question or challenge.

I didn't question it either, that is until my drunken insecurities got the best of me. Since starting the business and dropping out of university I felt I needed to prove to others that I was doing the right thing. When those insecurities were mixed with alcohol, the results were at times catastrophic.

One night, I cornered Rebecca and we began to get into a heated debate over the right choices to make in life. Alcohol fueled, I was on my high horse, trying hard to convince everyone that my life was amazing, that I had made the right choices and that university, which she was still studying at, was a scam. As are many who follow the medical profession, she was very proud and took her commitment to the Hippocratic oath seriously. I had goaded her enough with my words, but she was standing her ground and challenged me on my position.

With each minute passing, I took another swig of my drink – adding a little more fuel to the insecure fire I was burning inside. The more I drank, the more garbage came out of my mouth. In that moment I lost all her respect and that of the others around me through my constant barrage towards her. Many of my friends were listening to the vile gibberish I was spewing and all had a right to walk out of my life.

On that day, I broke a good friendship – a break that for the past 10 years has strained my relationship with others and left a sour taste in my heart since I have begun to realise and take responsibility for my actions. We've likely all been there when drinking – our words can cut like daggers. At the time I was unaware of my own struggles and was desperately trying to convince others I was okay. In doing so I cut off a friendship, something I am sorry for. This is the first of many stories in this book when I speak openly and in detail about the path of destruction I created – and is in fact the first time I have ever told some of these stories.

Rebeeca, if you're reading this, at the time you didn't realise but you were speaking to someone who was so broken inside they were fighting desperately to bring everyone else down to their level; a level that was far below yours and the pride you rightly have for your achievements. Over the past 10 years I have witnessed – albeit from afar – the person you've gone on to be and I have to say you did it. You achieved what you set out to do and you should be incredibly proud of it. I hope what that version of me said that evening didn't maim you and that you rose above it with the grace and elegance you always portrayed.

What I've learned is that words can do more damage than you imagine. Sometimes words are more dangerous than a punch. If you get punched, you may get a bruise but within days your skin will recover. The wrong words have the power to make someone else question their entire existence and can therefore cause much more long-term damage.

When building any new relationships, be they friendships or romantic relationships, there's a balance we all try to strike in terms of how much of our true selves we let others see and how quickly we open ourselves up. Alcoholics, who we know are masters of deflection, try to avoid showcasing the drunk versions of themselves when meeting someone new. But eventually the drunk version comes to the fore. As I've just shared, alcoholics ruin friendships through their behaviour. Of course they also ruin their romantic relationships. Research shows marriages end in divorce 50% of the time when one spouse drinks heavily.[1] The bottom line is relationships and alcohol do not go well together.

GATEWAYS

The consumption of alcohol (frequently referred to as a gateway drug) leads to drunken actions, which I'll refer to as gateway actions. In many cases, these are actions that no normal person would do when they were sober. These gateway actions go against the fundamental foundations of relationships. Gateway actions happen when that little voice in your mind starts to take over. Your actions in the short term are not conducive to achieving your long-term ambitions. We know the impact gateway drugs can have, leading you to use more dangerous and damaging substances. Gateway actions have the same impact on your behaviour. You start, you get away with it, and a reinforcement cycle is built. When I was drunk, some of alcohol's gateway actions led me to weaken my relationships.

Gateway action number 1: Speaking to and texting other people. This primarily applies to romantic relationships, but depending on who you inappropriately message, it has the power to destroy friendships too. Never in a sober state would I think this would be a smart thing to do while in a relationship. But drunk me has been there – in a bar and seen an Instagram story from a good-looking someone of the opposite sex and replied with emojis. This is attention seeking, and for some people it is where cheating starts. What could be seen as an innocent tap is the start of the rabbit hole of what the drunk version of you wants.

Gateway action number 2: Lying. Relationships of all kinds are built on a foundation of trust and the consequences of breaking that trust can be incredibly detrimental for any relationship. Alcohol makes you a liar – you lie about how long you were out last night, you lie about how much you had to drink last night, you lie about who you hung out with last night, you lie about how much you spent last night. These are all lies we tell ourselves, our partners, our friends and our families in situations in which alcohol has played a role.

Gateway action number 3: Aggression. This never happened to me, but I know many people to whom it did, and many people have suffered from this. We all know that one friend or one person who has a drink and suddenly wants to go 10 rounds with Mike Tyson.

They are unable to hold their tongue and they act up – putting themselves and their friends in danger. No one wants to see someone they care about not being able to control their emotions and reacting aggressively. I remember a friend and I once shouting something – I couldn't even tell you what – at two guys on the street as we were walking home after a night out. They chased us and in the process of running away from them, my mate tripped, face planted the floor and cut his chin. All because while we were drunk we thought shouting something would be funny.

Gateway action number 4: Reckless decision making. When I was younger, I once broke into a stadium. To get in, I had to climb a wall with anti-climb paint, cross walls with spikes and even barbed wire. In a sober state that would never have seemed like a sound idea to me, but drunk I thought it would be 'a laugh'. I was lucky I didn't get hurt, but this kind of poor decision making while drunk can lead to very serious consequences.

Particularly when you're younger, you can feel like you're immortal, but these things can lead to serious injuries or even death.

Gateway actions are the first steps towards true chaos and serious misdemeanours. While we're drunk, we might feel like we get away with these gateway actions and that increases the likelihood of committing even more regrettable actions.

SEEING OTHER PERSPECTIVES

One of my big issues while drinking was that I told myself that many of my insecurities could be solved with sex – albeit only for a short period of time. But while alcohol might have given me the confidence to talk to women I found attractive, it certainly didn't help the situation if they reciprocated and showed an interest in me.

Who can really hold their hands up and admit that when they had drunken sex, this was the best thing to ever happen to them?

I for one cannot say that I put in a good performance after a few red wines. I became selfish, self-centred and certainly wasn't an attentive partner. I'm not proud of this behaviour, or the fact that Drunk Dom used sex as an additional coping mechanism. When I reflect on relationships I had while I was drinking, I can probably count on a single hand the people I experienced joyful sex with where alcohol wasn't involved. You'd need many hands to count the alcohol-fuelled experiences on.

There have been a number of books written by people I deeply admire in the sober space about 'sober sex' and their experience of 'drunk sex', but I haven't read one from a male's perspective.

As a straight man, I can't speak to women's experiences in this area, nor those of people in the LGBTQ+ community. That said, I'm very aware there are major differences between my experiences and those of women and those in the LGBTQ+ community. It's important that all these perspectives are heard, because alcohol abuse can affect anyone.

As a man, I can never appreciate how different women's experiences are to mine in many areas of life, but I feel it's important here to digress and talk a bit about the differences that men and women experience while drinking. While alcohol, addiction, and other diseases do not discriminate, there are a lot of social differences between the sexes. I can only ever speak from my own experience, but over the past few years I have heard stories from women who I deeply respect about issues they have faced while drinking. One such person is Millie Gooch, founder of the Sober Girl Society, who spoke to me about some of the differences between the sexes.

MILLIE GOOCH, FOUNDER OF THE SOBER GIRL SOCIETY

I stopped drinking when I was 26. Although I wasn't a daily drinker, I was a blackout binge drinker – I couldn't stop once I'd started. I started drinking heavily when I went to university and that carried on into my early

20s. This was when I started struggling with my mental health and then drinking to get through it.

I suffer from blackouts when I'm drinking – I don't mean passing out, but having periods of a night out where I don't remember anything. I wish there had been more education about this when I was at school, rather than a focus on the physical harms of alcohol like cirrhosis. Blackouts in particular are such a messy, grey area – especially when it comes to consent, with some people believing that any alcohol consumed should actually void consent entirely.

When I look back to some of the situations I ended up in while drinking, it scares me. It scared me at the time, too. As Dom has mentioned, women's experiences when drunk can be, and often are, very different to men's. Getting home safely isn't a given.

There was one night in particular that sticks in my mind for all the wrong reasons. I woke up with a terrible hangover, sick on my clothes, and no idea how I'd got home to Kent from a night out in London. As I mentioned, one of my issues while drinking was that I'd experience periods of blackout. All I could remember were bits of the beginning of my night, but then nothing.

I'd been out in Covent Garden and needed to get to King's Cross to get the train home, so I looked at my Uber history to see if that could shed any light. I had got an Uber, but had been chucked out halfway through the journey. I had no cash on me and I could see I hadn't used my card. I looked up where the Uber had dropped me off – it was on a dark corner next to an NCP car park.

I started getting weird flashes of memory, of standing on a dark corner next to an eerie, empty car park and crying. It was horrendous and to this day I still have no idea how I made it safely from that corner back to my home. In all honesty I try not to think about it too much. But this became a common occurrence – I would put myself in situations where I got so drunk I couldn't remember how I got home.

My mum was constantly worried I was going to be kidnapped, because I couldn't drink sensibly and it just got out of control. She would often ask me not to get too drunk, but I never listened – like many 19–22 year olds, I thought I knew better.

There was one night when I was 19 which I'm sure only made my mum worry more. I was going home after a night out at university and got dropped off at the bus stop outside my house, where I still lived with my mum. I didn't want to go home though, so I phoned my boyfriend at the time and said I'd come to his place. He told me to stay where I was because I was really drunk and he'd come to me. After making that call, I passed out at the bus stop.

An off-duty police officer driving past saw me and pulled over to help. He tried to wake me up, and I started yelling and shouting so loudly that my mum heard and literally dragged me inside. She was furious with me and kept pointing out how lucky I was that it was an off-duty police officer who'd stopped and that anyone could have bundled me into their car.

Those are just a couple of examples of the kinds of situations I ended up in as a result of my drinking. Neither of those incidents alone made me question my relationship with alcohol, but this consistent pattern of behaviour became impossible to ignore.

The problem with drinking alcohol, for men and women, is that it affects our prefrontal cortex, which is responsible for rational decision making. As soon as you drink, it makes it harder to make rational decisions – such as drinking responsibly. You reach a point of myopic thinking, where all you can think about is the here and now; you don't think about the consequences for tomorrow, or even a few hours later.

The alcohol industry has made it our "responsibility" to regulate our consumption of what we know to be an addictive substance, even when there is mountains of evidence to show that consuming that substance makes us less likely to behave responsibly. Even if you don't drink so much you black out, having alcohol in your system can affect your decisions – like a decision to walk home on your own rather than getting a taxi. Personally alcohol led to too many poor decisions on my part, and I've learned that complete abstinence is the right route for me.

Other people might think differently – some people can have the occasional drink and don't have an urge to keep going. Whether you become fully sober, or just moderate your alcohol consumption is a personal choice. All I would say is that anyone can benefit from drinking less. It's important to get to know yourself and to be okay with what works for you. This is what I describe as a mindful, harm reductionist view on alcohol consumption.

Making the change

In my early 20s I got into a really destructive cycle of drinking heavily, doing some really stupid things, and not remembering any of it the next day. For a while I told myself I was a party girl, that I was fine and this was just what I did. But when I got to 26 I realised I couldn't go on like this. I knew I needed to sort my life out or I was going to fall into a full-blown addiction. That was when I decided to stop drinking.

But I felt like I needed some support, and recovery programmes like AA didn't feel like the right fit for me. It was as though you were either alcohol dependent, or everything was fine. There was no middle ground. I didn't feel as though I was alcohol dependent, but I also didn't know how to socialise without alcohol. There wasn't much available to help people like me, who were trying to navigate social situations, work events and many other occasions without an alcoholic drink in hand.

That was when I started writing about sobriety, as well as following people on Instagram who were active in the sobriety space. This led to me founding the Sober Girl Society in 2018, which now runs events and meetups all over the UK for anyone who is struggling with getting sober, or just sober curious. The aim of the community is to help people navigate all kinds of social situations without alcohol, provide support for anyone who wants to change their relationship with alcohol, and help people see that sobriety doesn't mean "no fun". We have a lot of fun!

You can learn more about us here: https://sobergirl society.com/

Now I'm going to share the same story from a male and female perspective. Let's start with what, in my eyes, would be a very funny story, if I heard about this from a male friend . . .

One of my friends got so drunk that he passed out on the train home and missed his stop. From the male perspective, this is actually funny, and when I heard the story I laughed. The story goes like this: Chris, one of my best friends and groomsmen at my wedding, lived in Leeds and came back to York for a night out with us all. He planned to get the last train home to Leeds at 12.40 am after our traditional '12 pubs of Christmas' – which we did on 23 December every year (so it's dark, and cold). The next day we debriefed in the group chat, on what happened and how nice it was to see each other.

Chris then popped up: "Guys, I fucked up last night."

With great anticipation we waited for what was going to come next . . .

"I feel asleep on the train and woke up in Dewsbury."

He continued, "There were no taxis because it's Christmas Eve. Trains had all finished and I had no idea what I should do, so I rang my mum to come get me from York" (a 2 hour round trip).

Well, the chat blew up with laughter, how funny was this? Chris had screwed up and accidentally ended up in a different city from where he lived a few days before Christmas. For context, Chris is 6' 3", hairy and in my opinion pretty damn ugly (love you). He is able to handle himself and wouldn't be an obvious target for anyone. Really, he isn't ever in much danger. In this situation – at 2.00 am, in a city he's never been to before, in the freezing cold winter, having to wait for an hour for his mum to pick him up – I'm pretty confident he never felt unsafe.

Now, imagine Chris was a 5' 3" female who I'll call Millie.

Millie works in London and commutes back home to Kent – she goes for drinks after work on a Thursday with friends and decides to get the last train home – in doing so she misses her stop, because she is so intoxicated that she passes out on the train journey. Now, it's the early hours of the morning, there are no trains back to her home and she has to get off at an unknown station and try to figure out a way to get home. I can't put myself in her shoes, but I can imagine that when this story is told the next day in the girls' WhatsApp chat that there isn't such a positive banter about the event. There is genuine danger here.

I have invested in a company called Walksafe, which shares data, insights, and location of 'city angels' to make it safer for people (mainly women) to get home safely. This was started in the wake of a number of significant disappearances of women including Sarah Everard.

Like Chris, I am also 6' 3", hairy and pretty damn ugly, so I've never read a headline about someone going missing on a night out, or being attacked and thought 'god that could have been me'. It's never occurred to me.

Remember my story about the night when I broke my ankle? My friends had become so accustomed to my disappearing that they didn't even question my not being around. In their minds, there was no risk – I am a big boy, I will be able to get myself home.

Having spoken to a number of women who go out frequently together, there is more panic when they lose someone on a night out – WhatsApp chats go wild. For example, Mille told me that one night she woke up with over 67 missed calls from friends and also her mum. (Millie's friends had her mum's number and were so worried that they woke up her mother as well.) I think the most missed calls I've ever woken up with were two or three. I don't think this is an indication that I have bad friends. I think there is less concern among men than women when one of us disappears on a night out, because for the most part, the potential risks we face as men are nowhere near as severe as the potential risks faced by women.

At the beginning of this section, I talked about sex, and how drunk sex was one of the ways I tried to boost my self-confidence. I had one-night stands, but never did I feel in any danger doing so. However, there is a vastly different outlook between men and women towards a one-night stand.

I have friends who have frequently woken up in a random person's flat, in some unknown part of town, having had one night of drunken fun with someone they didn't know. Now, let's look at the risks for young men in this situation:

§ you could get an STI, and
§ you could get the woman pregnant.

I think those are the main risks for men, and the second one isn't as big a risk to a man as it is to a woman.

Having spoken to many women about their experiences, I've realised waking up in a stranger's house with no idea where you are, how you are going to get home, or what happened last night, is a much scarier proposition. Big questions with possibly life-changing consequences are: Did we have sex? Did I consent? Did we use protection?

Millie told me a story about when she went out, ended up hooking up with a guy and going back to his place. He left her in the morning to go to work and told her "My flat mate is downstairs, he will let you out." Now, there's a danger: who is this guy? Not to mention how embarrassing the whole situation is.

When alcohol is involved, you risk removing all inhibitions and rational decision making, which can put you in dangerous circumstances. We see it in the media and when something happens the reaction in the tabloids is often, "they were drunk". I've read this over and over again – but there is no fault on the victim other than being in the wrong place at the wrong time.

Millie's mother's biggest concern was one day "she would get abducted" – a fear my own mother never expressed to me. Imagine the worry of sleeping at night, thinking as a parent "what trouble are they going to get into?" Even if you know your son or daughter is usually responsible, as Millie pointed out we are all aware that alcohol can lead to poor decision making, or even just mean we let our guard down with the wrong person.

From speaking with my own mother about the trouble I would get into, the biggest worry she had was that I'd get into a fight, which can result in a 'one punch kill', something that has been seen in a number of circumstances.

I read a very powerful story about Jacob Dunne.[2] Jacob Dunne had a penchant for engaging in fights, often heading into Nottingham city centre with friends to stir up trouble. During a summer night in 2011, at 19 years old, he threw a single punch that felt oddly distinct. There was no push-back, and the person he hit staggered without resistance. "I sensed something wasn't right as soon as I struck him", he reflects today. Without a word to his companions, Dunne swiftly fled the scene.

As weeks passed, he put the incident out of his mind. Surely, if something dire had occurred, he would have heard about it. Yet, friends who were present that night contacted him; they had been questioned about the alter-cation. It seemed inevitable that he would soon be sought out. Indeed, accusations were already being directed at him. He learned that one of his friends had disclosed his name to the police.

Then, one day, the police showed up at his mother's residence. Since he wasn't home, they contacted him and requested he surrender himself for questioning – nothing, they assured him, of grave concern. Upon arriving at the police station, however, he found himself arrested on suspicion of murder. Dunne was shocked to learn that the man he had struck, 28-year-old trainee paramedic James Hodgkinson, had passed away after spending nine days in a coma. The worry for my parents was always that I would be the one getting punched or doing the punching.

Alternatively, they likely worried that I would do 'something stupid', like jumping into a river. At the age of 18, I was unfortunate enough to watch in York as Paul Rogerson fell into the icy water of the River Ouse and slowly dropped under the water.[3] To this day, I wish I could have done something about it. My mother has four boys, I deeply believe her worries were different from a mother of four girls. While these are horrendous situations, as a guy they weren't things I actively worried about. From what I've heard from the women I've spoken to, that's the major difference. Women actively worry about being sexually assaulted, attacked or abducted. While alcohol in itself is not the cause of any of those things, they are aware that being drunk makes them less able to defend themselves.

MY SPIRAL OF SELF-DIAGNOSIS

Let's pick my story up again. It's 3 June, and I've woken up with a broken ankle after falling through what was the last glass bottom – an experience that for someone else could have been enough for them to stop drinking, to change their habits and to act as a wakeup call for them – but not for me. Little did I know that I had further to go and harder to hit. At that point in my life, the wake-up calls had played only a small role in changing my attitude towards my relationship with alcohol. I had repeatedly made a fool of myself and taken my actions too far, and I had a semi-conscious understanding that maybe I needed to make a change. After this latest glass bottom, not only had the falls started to be mentally and physically more damaging but the frequency had increased and become more consistent. I was looking at a damaging situation every week or two. There started to be comments and suggestions from others that this was becoming too much. I felt this undercurrent and I felt I needed to respond to it – I needed to make a change in my life to stabilise this, at least in the short term. I began the dangerous and lonely route of self-diagnosing.

The first thing I determined was causing me problems was the drugs. I hadn't touched drugs until I was 22, but I'd started experimenting with other substances to help create the sense of numbness I was seeking and to help me escape my reality. So, my first self-experiment was to begin removing drugs from my nights out. Obviously in this decision-making process there is some rationality. I knew some other major screw up was coming. I knew and felt that something I was going to do could be serious, so I told myself I needed to bring stability to my life.

The second action plan I set myself on was to create some security in my personal life. I had always enjoyed having a partner – having someone to share experience with. Part of this was self-validation and potentially filling a hole in myself that I could have filled myself with hard work, therapy and healing – but at the time finding some stability and removing the wanderlust felt important and I believed that a serious relationship would bring what I was looking for. I was pretty early into seeing someone – still to this day, I couldn't tell you if we were seriously committed, but I knew I wanted to be.

So this was my start – the two things I thought would heal me: rushing into a serious relationship with someone and stopping taking drugs. What could possibly go wrong? Self-diagnosing people often seek information that confirms their beliefs or preconceived notions, and I focused on information that supported my opinion and ignored contradictory evidence. I believed that I was at last really happy with myself, that I had the self-esteem I wanted, the confidence I sought and all-around general happiness in life that I had when I was last in a good stable healthy relationship – back in 2013. This failed to take into account the changing life situation I had experienced, which had led to the problems that were causing me to drink in the first place, so while trying to fill a void feels like it can solve a problem, it cannot. I have heard this too many times in my experience professionally – when someone is unhappy at work, there are a number of factors that could be causing them discomfort in a position.

There could be underlying reasons, like personal matters, which are impacting them. However, we tend to make a decision to change jobs because we see it as a solution to our problems. Without addressing the core reason for our unhappiness, however, our problems are rarely solved. The easiest things to change tend not to be the major things impacting our lives. We can travel to Australia for a new job, new life, new career but our deepest, darkest thoughts come with us on the plane. We may be able to bury our heads in the sand for a short period of time and experience a new-scenario bounce where being with new people in a new environment can mask those issues, but at some point they will catch up with you and you'll find yourself stopping to think and realising that the changes you need to make aren't just packing up and moving. The real change has to come from within you, not your surroundings.

I know this, perhaps I even knew it back then. But during this period of self-diagnosis I began to question whether I'd be better off without my business, without everything I had spent the past 3 years building. I began to believe my own bullshit that this was actually what was causing me the problems. The anxiety, stress and everything in between from the business was too much for me and therefore leaving it was the change I had to make.

One of the factors that influenced this was our first major acquisition conversations. The Hut Group (THG), a company that was quickly becoming the North West poster boy for its rapid growth, innovation, and culture, was sweeping up businesses left, right, and centre and headcount was growing almost 500% year on year. It was becoming the place to be and the company to work for. As a marketing business we had been desperately trying to work with them – they dominated the beauty and fitness sector with some of their brands. We knew working with them would be a major coup.

From 24 May 2016 – in the middle of the storm I had already created for myself – we began discussions over a major acquisition or investment into our company. Now, these things are not easy to manage, and this is not something that comes across your desk every day. This fell onto my desk during my darkest days, but I took it upon myself to lead the project. To say I wasn't ready is a major understatement.

On the surface, we were a match made in heaven – we had built an efficient service business working with some of the world's largest companies. At this point we could reference Disney, Spotify, 21st Century Fox, and Apple as some of our clients. The bunch of kids controlling social media and influencing what other kids are talking about have grown up. THG is a new-age commerce business, which had mastered performance channels and were looking to improve their capabilities in the areas we specialised in. This could have been perfect, but there were a few major issues we discovered going through the process. At this point we were still young and naive – no one had ever asked for 'our numbers', we had never really needed to produce management accounts, a detailed cash flow forecast for the next 5 years, or propose our own M&A strategy and internationalisation plans. Only 2 years previously we were kids in Thailand enjoying our lives and now we were being stretched in major corporate discussions at only 23. Here I am on one hand speaking about how I was abusing my body with substances, drinking to forget the pain, breaking my ankle on a Thursday night and all these other ridiculous things, while in parallel I was going through what is potentially a life-changing discussion for the business. Can you imagine how much of a fraud I felt?

While trying to understand our business model, I, alongside our advisors, learnt more about our company than I could have imagined. The questions I was asked, while difficult, also were the questions we should have been asking ourselves. But when your time is spent putting out fires and disasters in the business, which occurred daily for us, we weren't able as founders to look forward and plan strategically, which fuelled the issues I was facing. As the conversations advanced I began to become fixated on the idea that this was my magic golden ticket to sail off into the sunset. Selling the company would get rid of all the problems I was facing at the time. I would be able to have the life I needed.

I can say with complete certainty that if that deal had gone ahead, and I was still drinking, I wouldn't be here today. I would be in a ditch somewhere with a washed-up life. There was no way this would have ended well for someone with the unstable foundations I had and who was granted the size of deal we had discussed. The only answer to that equation was a catastrophe, which might have made the front pages of my local newspaper.

But my self-diagnosis knew no limits. I was looking at every possible angle to try to land on something that would fix the issues inside myself – none of which, I remind you, I had any idea about. But the looks and comments people began to make about my actions were becoming noticeable.

There were throwaway comments of, "no doubt you'll be heading out this weekend", or an all-time classic, "drinking in the office again, Dom?" – maybe this was my saving grace – noticing that these little remarks were building up traction. Even if my self-diagnosis was deeply flawed, I was at least acknowledging there was a problem, even if I was avoiding the biggest problem of all. However, the period of A/B testing (split or bucket testing) my actions that my self-diagnosis led to was, and remains, the most destructive period of my journey to rock bottom.

I tried my first A/B test – not taking drugs. While this on the surface sounds like a sensible first move and something that could have a major positive effect on an individual, for me – for any addict – it wouldn't.

As mentioned earlier in this book, I believe my connection to alcohol was formed very early in the emotional period of celebrating, praising, and commiserating. Alcohol had become my mood regulator. So when one of these moments occurred and my emotional base was unbalanced, I'd try to balance that out with another shot of Sambuca. So, deep down, how did my alcohol-addicted brain view not taking drugs on a night out? Well, it was an achievement, a success, something to celebrate. While sober, Dom could make the sensible decision not to buy any substances, therefore making it harder for Drunk Dom to use them. Drunk Dom then wanted to reward himself for not consuming any of the substances. What was the emotional reward Drunk Dom wanted? . . . More alcohol. So by removing drugs from my social settings, I unintentionally drank even more than I normally would. Based on my recent history, I can say there are no benefits to this. Which night did I conduct this test? The opening of Neighbourhood, 2 June. You already know how that went. My short-lived A/B testing had failed.

LOOKING FOR LOVE

The other thing I'd determined through my self-diagnosis was that I would be better off if I was in a serious relationship. At this time, I was seeing a 27-year-old called Olivia. She was running her own business, lived in Liverpool and was very attractive. We had a lot of fun when we were together, usually focused on drinking. Because she was in Liverpool and I was in Manchester, we didn't see each other all the time. That meant I was able to hide the worst of my drinking relatively easily, and be 'fun Drunk Dom' when we were together.

That said, our relationship was not one that was built on strong foundations. I felt she was out of my league and my confidence at the time was pretty low – through the months of drinking through days and evenings I had seen my weight balloon. Not only that, but as alcohol changes the way you look, the other main problems that impacted me were puffy eyes and dark circles around the eyes caused by water retention. You start to look more like a racoon than a human. The puffiness of the eyes almost extended to my cheeks.

Today I am 30 and I show people pictures of me during this period and they cannot recognise me. I am frequently told I look younger now than I did then. Slowly the alcohol had changed my appearance. I was also impacted by major skin problems, significant facial redness, and constantly looking flushed. The weight gain through the excessive calories, tiredness leading to a lack of movement, and the desire to eat unhealthy food meant that I was not only in the worst mental state of my life – I was in the worst physical state of my life. There was nothing left of the 20 year old who ran his first marathon in less than 4 hours just 3 years ago.

This low level of self-esteem led me to make a number of illogical decisions during mine and Olivia's relationship that ultimately pushed her away. I was so desperate for something to work – but in the end things fizzled out and we went our separate ways. As it turned out, this was a twist of fate that changed my luck in relationships, and changed my life.

Towards the end of my relationship with Olivia, Georgie started working at the company as an intern. We had an instant connection, not that anything romantic happened between us at this point. We were colleagues, we got on, and we both sensed the attraction, but neither of us acted on it. I later learned that her last relationship had been with someone who drank a lot, and she had had some very bad experiences with him.

When we did decide to start dating, Georgie and I were very aware of how our relationship might appear to others. I never wanted to be the person who had a one-night stand with someone at the office, let alone someone I managed. Although I was "the boss", she is actually 1 year and 1 week older than me. I spoke to Steve about it and he told me that both he and the company as a whole were fine with us starting a relationship, as long as it was serious – a story he reminded us of in his best man's speech at my wedding.

This choice became a crucial crossroads in my life. There were many reasons why mine and Georgie's relationship might not have worked out – working together or my drinking could both have ended things for us.

Although I had yet to acknowledge my issues with alcohol, Georgie had strict boundaries, which she made very clear to me once we did start dating – roughly one month before I went sober. This was one of the first times

I remember someone standing up to me and telling me "no" in relation to alcohol. Although I talked a lot about how great it was to have freedom, be my own boss and not have others telling me what to do, part of me was crying out for structure.

When I was dating Olivia, there was never a "no". We used to have 'tequila Sundays', or go on weekends away in Europe and get hideously drunk. That changed with Georgie, and as I'll explain later, having her in my life made a huge difference to the success of my recovery.

As I mentioned earlier, CEOs and founders can live a very lonely life. That is where I believed I had reached. Real loneliness. Not loneliness in how people normally perceive it. This was a loneliness in which you look at your peers, your family, your friends and think 'no one here knows the shit I am dealing with right now'. That single line, which I repeated to myself over and over again, was the driver in never opening up to anyone – I thought no one would care, or understand. So meeting people while suffering from this type of loneliness was very difficult. Then, as the company's profile rises, you become paranoid over people's intentions – will they like you for who you are or are they more interested in the trips to Rome for the Bank Holiday weekend?

By this stage, my time was either spent in the office, or drunk. There was no in-between. In the office, there were days when I could be myself, days when I had that glow to myself – and was the person I knew I could be. The great creative ideas, the problem-solving ability, people who saw me around the office as Sober Dom – saw something they could believe in and support. It also meant that I could portray the best version of myself to Georgie. I wasn't just a drunk mess, I had great traits, some positive. There was hope, but I had a lot of work to do and Drunk Dom was busy destroying Sober Dom's life.

ALCOHOL AS A DRUG

Now, I want to talk about alcohol as a drug. I know of many people who see alcohol as significantly less damaging than, say, MDMA, cocaine or weed. By definition, one of them is legal while the others you can face court proceedings for carrying on your person. The classification of drugs is a complex matter and alcohol has been around since before records began.

In fact, the earliest evidence of an alcoholic drink comes from 7000–6000 BCE in China, archaeologists have found pottery that hints at fermented drinks from that period.[4] It is an integral part of human history and culture. We can see that in many religions. For example, in Christianity, when the taking of Mass occurs, wine is used to symbolise the blood of Christ. Therefore for almost 2000 years Christendom – which is the foundation of modern Europe – has used wine in their major religious weekly service.

There are also entire economic centres of the world that are fundamentally based on the production of alcoholic drinks. The Champagne Region in France, rosé from Provence, beer from Germany, Belgium and the Netherlands, vodka from Russia – you name it, the history of alcoholic drinks is very closely linked to local history from countries across the world. In the United Kingdom we have a crazy history and relationship with gin. After the Thirty Years' War with the Netherlands, soldiers brought gin to the United Kingdom, and this spirit became incredibly popular with the working class. This led to the 'gin craze' in the 18th century United Kingdom creating a period of huge gin consumption. This was driven by unlicensed distilleries throughout the country mainly in impoverished urban areas. They were producing cheap, low-quality gin – the stuff that could make you blind. As it was cheap and easy to get, it was attractive mainly to the working class and of course, this led to a major knock-on impact causing huge social problems. The excessive consumption of gin (and probably other forms of alcohol as well) led to an increase of crime, poverty and public disorder across many parts of the United Kingdom. This resulted in the Gin Act of 1736, which regulated the sale of gin and imposed high licensing fees and regulation on sales.

The Gin Act of 1736 was repealed in 2008. Then in 2009 Sipsmith won a battle against HMRC to produce gin in smaller quantities rather than industrial ones – this is what opened the door to Liverpool Gin, Didsbury Gin, Edinburgh Gin, and all the other local gins that have hit the global shelves since then. This has led to the latest 'gin craze' in which, by October 2018 alone, Brits bought almost 55 million bottles, up 44% from the same period in 2017. That's 1.32 billion gin and tonics.[5] This cultural–historical tie goes some way to explain how integrated alcohol is into our lives and into our social and cultural activities in the

United Kingdom. For every Gin Act of 1736 there are other historical efforts to ban or limit the sale of alcohol – most significantly the American Prohibition from 1920 to 1933. The experiment failed and since then alcohol has poured freely across the USA.

Drugs, on the other hand, are not so readily available. Though that hasn't always been the case. Many of them are chemically manufactured, like cocaine, which began as medicine and gained popularity as a famous drink: Coca-Cola. Despite these original purposes, cocaine was swiftly classified as a Schedule II controlled substance in the United States due to the potential for abuse and negative health effects, thus driving the practice underground, or as many young people know, to WhatsApp chats and back-street pickups. In 2023, I saw a menu to order anything you wanted from LSD to pills that would be delivered to your doorstep in 10 minutes – an infrastructure that would rival delivery giants like Amazon.

In the United Kingdom, our relationship with alcohol on a societal level is complicated. On the one hand, we know it causes problems. On the other hand, we choose to ignore them so we can keep drinking. This is not dissimilar to how I saw my relationship with alcohol before I stopped drinking. Cutting out illegal drugs was easier than not drinking alcohol because drugs were not a part of my daily life and not as ubiquitous in society as a whole. What I hadn't yet realised was that alcohol was the drug that I had the biggest problem with, but that realisation was coming.

NOTES

1. *Heavy drinking is bad for marriage if one spouse drinks, but not both.* (2013, November 3). University at Buffalo. https://www.buffalo.edu/news/releases/2013/11/031.html

2. Simon Hattenstone (2022). The man who killed a stranger with a single punch, and then turned his life around. *The Guardian.* https://www.theguardian.com/society/2022/may/14/knew-bad-as-soon-as-hit-him-man-who-killed-a-stranger-with-single-punch-then-turned-his-life-around

3. Kate Liptrot (2021). River victim Paul Rogerson fell off bridge parapet. *York Press.* https://www.yorkpress.co.uk/news/8952059.river-victim-paul-rogerson-fell-off-bridge-parapet/

4. Wikipedia contributors (2023, December 26). *History of alcoholic drinks.* Wikipedia. https://en.wikipedia.org/wiki/History_of_alcoholic_drinks#cite_note-21

5. Elsie Taylor (2018). How gin bounced back from decades of decline to become London's latest it drink. *Vogue.* https://www.vogue.com/article/how-gin-became-londons-it-drink-again

CHAPTER 4

THE FINAL FALL

As I hurtled towards what would be my fall to rock bottom, I think one of the craziest parts about this scenario is that no one had any idea of the degree of my struggling – over the months leading up to July 2016, I had started to contemplate suicide. Now, I know this is a very delicate and triggering subject for many, and that many people have had exposure to this horrible situation – myself included. I can only talk from my own perspective and the statistics and data that are out there in our world. The scariest statistic for me is that, as a 30-year-old man, the most likely way I am going to die is by suicide. It's the most common cause of death for men under the age of 45 in England and Wales.[1] Globally over 700,000 people die by suicide every year.[2] That means one every 40 seconds, so since you started reading this paragraph, someone else has unfortunately died by suicide.

That also means any male you know under 45 – if they were to die, it would be more likely to be self-inflicted than any other cause. This is terrifying, and as someone who managed to make a dramatic change in my life to avoid this path, there were a few meaningful reasons that managed to pull my mind back from ever acting on the eternal sleep that I was craving.

I had all the characteristics of a suicide profile. First, I was suffering in silence, I had not spoken to anyone about what I was going through, my drinking was my "cry for help". The only evidence was the dramatic change in my personality, which you could see from an external view of my life, but I had done as much as I could to hide it from people. Second, I was struggling with my mental and physical health. I had no financial or money issues, but I had doubt and uncertainty over my future. But most significantly, I had mentally rehearsed how I would end my life.

The research on suicide shows that the likelihood of going through with it increases once an individual decides on the method of suicide they will use[3] and that's what I had done. In my mind, I knew what I wanted to do – on my normal commute to London, a place I associated with work and therefore strain and stress, I knew that one morning instead of getting on that train to face and deal with the problems I had, I would jump in front of the train and finally get the silence my head was craving.

There were a number of times I stood over the yellow line that station staff make you stand behind when a train is approaching. As the train came past and I felt the rush of air from the carriages, it almost gave me a slight buzz, a feeling of being alive. I've never been one to follow rules and in these moments standing behind the yellow line was just one rule I couldn't follow. I would think to myself, "What would happen if I jumped in front of the 7.11 from Wilmslow to

London? I would be okay, wouldn't I?" To this moment I don't know if the feeling of "I would be okay" was down to the fact that my problems would have gone away or if I was deluded enough to believe that jumping in front of a train travelling at over 200 miles per hour would leave me with no visible damage. I lean towards the former.

I think I believed that my problems would end and that, like the night I crawled to bed with a broken ankle, I would have the sleep I was so desperately seeking. At that time in my life I was getting the train to London about twice a week, so the idea was well manifested in my mind. It would require minimum effort, just one extra step than I would usually take, past the yellow line and into – what I thought would be bliss.

Although this was obviously an accessible method of suicide for me, I don't believe that was the only reason jumping in front of train came to my mind. My first job when I was 18 was working in a coffee shop at York Station. I would wake up at 4.30 am to meet the morning rush hour of business-like people going to London, Leeds, or Edinburgh. My role in their lives was to serve them coffee. I always wondered what life would be like on the other side of the counter. A few years later I found out, as I was the one getting a coffee to take to the platform. As well as a coffee, I was carrying a crushing weight on my shoulders, not having any tools or techniques for how to handle this and thinking the easiest thing to do would be to check out of the journey before even getting onto the train.

While working around the station, I learned from the conductors and those working on the railways what would happen after a 'jumper' occurred on the tracks. In my few months at the coffee shop this must have happened at least four or five times. I remember asking Darren, one of the conductors who I got to know well, about what happened to the jumper. He only ever said, "It would be instant." This feeling must have stuck with me all those years, and I felt that it would be quick, simple and effectively painless.

At this point, I am reminded of a famous quote about change (that I believe is by Tony Robbins). It has always stuck with me:

Change happens when the pain of staying the same is greater than the pain of change.[4]

The reason I never stepped out and took that pain of change was because I had some hope left. I was holding onto glimmers of hope, which meant that even in my worst moments I was able to rationalise with the voice that was edging me towards the end of the platform. I could tell it that at this moment, it wasn't the right time to take that step.

Do I understand why someone might consider suicide? Yes.

Do I think that was the pathway for which I could have headed? Yes.

Do I think that I would be here today if I hadn't stopped drinking? No.

I was desperately looking for an answer to my problems, and at this point the only method I had to even attempt to manage my emotions was with alcohol.

At the time I was in my early 20s, running an award-winning business, somewhere considered one of the best places to work, and my life was just beginning. No one I was standing near on that platform or who knew me would ever have considered that when I got to the station for my commute, the first thing that crossed my mind when I saw the train was – "God, I wish I could jump out in front of it."

A DAY AT THE RACES

By now it's July 2016. I was still drinking and these thoughts of suicide were a regular occurrence. When you look at the recipes for an extreme disaster for an alcoholic like I was, there are a few elements that will create potential chaos. The first is a free bar, the second is unstable personal circumstances, and the third is a safe, non-judgemental environment. I didn't know when I woke up on 23 July that this would be the day that would lead me to never drink again. I believe that's part of the worry – when you're in a downhill spiral, you don't really see the spiral, you don't know you are approaching the bottom. The day starts like any normal day, you wake up, you get ready, and you have your first drink of the day – like you have hundreds of times before.

My 'last supper' of drinking was at Chester Racecourse at an annual meet, hosted by a spread betting company, in one of the boxes right on the finishing line with 12 other individuals – only one of them I knew (kind of); the other 11 were complete strangers. As we arranged ourselves around the table there was no preconception of who I was, what I was like when I was drunk, or what I had done previously, so there was no possibility of judgement. There was also only a very small chance that I'd see any of these individuals in my life ever again, so the chances of any consequences coming back and biting me were extremely low. I could drown my sorrows, feed my demons, batter my body and carry on with this aggressive disease that had slowly taken over my life. This was a situation it would thrive from.

I had been invited into a box, offering 'all you can drink, all you can eat', and a part of me perceived this as the rockstar life and felt I was living it. But the day was heading to a relatively sour note: six races in and I had lost every bet I made.

I gave myself a £700 budget just to throw away at horses – or £100 a race. But, my rational sober brain didn't take into account how much I would chase my losses. By the time the final race came about at 5.30 pm, I was unable to hold a conversation, unable to walk, the prestige suit I had worn was slowly unravelling, my tie was all over the place, my shirt was untucked, and the only thing to hide my shame were the sunglasses on my face, which were hiding my bloodshot eyes. Having lost every race so far, I can still remember my inner dialogue calling myself a failure and saying what a waste this afternoon has been. There was a feeling in me that I needed something to change the day – I was beating myself up for losing bets, wasting money, all while the alcohol was fuelling the monster inside me. Every drop of the red wine poured into my glass was quickly thrown down my throat with no consideration for anything other than the here and now. I gave no thought to the fact that I was later meeting people from the office, or to what the repercussions would be. There is nothing but selfishness when drunk, and an inability to think about the long term.

Research into drinking shows that consuming alcohol lowers your inhibitions,[5] potentially altering your behaviours and leading to negative outcomes. Impaired judgement, though difficult to quantify, can lead you to engage in risky behaviours and to poor outcomes for your health and social standing. This is where I was, everything was just about this moment, getting the next drink inside me and trying to figure out a way to recover my lost money.

At that point in my life, I never had to really think or worry about money. I know how privileged this is, and it had quickly become the life I was living. But even though I didn't need the money, Drunk Dom didn't want to be a loser, he didn't want to walk away from the table when he was down. I was unable to say to myself, "this is enough now."

While this story contains truths about the effects of alcohol, the knock-on impact goes into other areas. When you are drunk your actions are different to those when you are sober. The things you say, the food you eat, the decisions you make, all of these are blurred by the toxins in your body, and although you have to take responsibility for them, you don't have full control over your choices when you make them.

Especially when you're intoxicated beyond control.

I did not want to leave the track a loser. Losing is something Drunk Dom won't tolerate, there is no way he is going to be belittled. I stumbled over to the bookmakers, tapped my card and placed £100 on the last race on a horse at 10 to 1. This was the last roll of the dice; this was the last chance to recoup and make a profit for the day.

There was no logic or insight behind my choice of horse; there was no tip – this was a drunk pointing at a horse and hoping for the best.

There's a famous British saying that goes, "win or lose, we're on the booze", and that's exactly where I was when I was at the track. So if this bet wins, I know what the outcome is going to be – I'll celebrate. If I win £1,100, my emotions will skyrocket and I'm going to feel untouchable, on a high and as though I own the world. If I walk away from a day £900 down at 5.30 pm, I am going to drown my sorrows until I am unable to stand.

I do not know which outcome, at this point, would be worse.

Looking back, the role luck has played in my story always seems to nudge me towards the best outcome for myself – maybe not in the moment, but in the long term.

"And they're off . . ."

The sound of the starter gun silenced the crowd, there were many others in my situation – others whose days were going to be determined by the outcome of a horse race. This is the same across all betting, and especially at horse races, you can feel the crowd as the day goes on getting more and more excited by the winner. This effect is twofold, mainly due to the increased consumption of booze, but also the desperation of losing throughout the day that leads to an overwhelming display of emotions 'if' the tables turn and you go on to be 'a winner'.

As the horses approached the final furlong, I was frantically trying to spot my horse, Number 16 . . . as they came towards the line there were a number of them still in contention. Given my desperation for a successful day, I had the horse to Win Only – again a rational brain would go 'each way' and not have an 'all-or-nothing' situation. That was it, it really was all or nothing.

This is a fascinating psychological phenomenon. My life had become very binary and I viewed things as all or nothing.[6] It is a cognitive distortion and a pattern of thought that most often is not based on facts. It may make you see your world more negatively than it really is. Here it was in action. With my blurred eyes and drunken hearing I wasn't able to see who won – I wasn't able to process the outcome or my bet. I had to do a double take of my ticket to remind myself which was my horse (as information at this point was going in, and swiftly out) when the screen across the course pops up with Number 16, the winner. . .

It had happened, I had won – luck once again had changed the trajectory of my day. But it didn't just change the trajectory of my day, it was about to change the trajectory of my entire life.

I wobbled on over to the counter to collect my cash, £1,100 in £20 notes. As the day's events at the racecourse had now concluded I stuck the £20 notes in my inside jacket pocket and made my way to the exit. I had arranged to meet Georgie, who I had now been effectively dating for the past month, and who had been to the races separately.

We were in the honeymoon phase of our relationship – just over 4 weeks, life here is supposed to be exciting and fun – real young love. It wasn't.

Out of the races walked this ogre of a man: cocky, arrogant, he'd just won big and felt untouchable. So my actions began to reflect that arrogance. The gateway actions began, and I was caught messaging another girl, who I know lived in Chester. The beast within me needed some validation. I wanted some attention that wasn't right in front of me – it was like an urge to destroy the blossoms of a relationship.

Georgie looked down at my screen and saw what I was doing – just as we got into a taxi.

On the taxi ride back my mind was spinning, the rejection she was giving me (all self-inflicted), and the alcohol started to hit – in the 40-minute ride home I entered the worst state of myself. A cocktail of emotions were swelling inside of me – the deep issues with work that had driven me to get mindlessly drunk, the fear of losing another relationship before it even started, and the arrogance of my drunken state thinking that I deserved better than this.

The cocktail began to bubble and it became a time bomb, which was now primed to go off . . . The only question was be – how much damage would I do, to myself and to others?

We were going to meet some of the team from the business who were at a planning session for our impending US launch – something that we had been working on now for the past few months.

The bomb was walking into this and there was only a small chance that this was going to end well.

As we approached the bar, the silence in the taxi was all I needed to know that I had lost Georgie's trust. I had pushed another good thing away. So I abruptly left the taxi to meet the team at the bar. I sat with them and demanded a drink from the waiters – in my state they refused to serve me, quite rightly. So I did what Drunk Dom thought was the next best thing: I decided to reach behind me, to a table of six women enjoying a nice afternoon drink in the sun, and grabbed their bottle of wine out of the cooling stand and began to pour it into my glass. In utter disbelief they were too shocked to even comment.

One of them broke the spell of disbelief, shouting, "What the f**k are you doing, mate!"

This was when everyone around me began to apologise. I reached into my pocket where all my cash was stored and threw a handful of £20 notes at them and told them to "shut up".

This wasn't me, this wasn't the usual behaviour of any sane individual.

Rightfully so, before I could finish drinking the glass of wine I had poured myself, the bouncers came over to eject us all from the restaurant.

I would not go quietly. Georgie and the team were planning on having a nice day – so kindly, Michael Heaven decided to try to negotiate with the bouncer that I would leave and he would take me.

Writing these words and thinking back on this is opening up deep trauma that I have never addressed privately, let alone publicly. Writing this is the first time I have openly spoken about what happened that afternoon.

Michael, who had been one of my closest friends for 4 years – he had joined the business, left his job and put his trust in what we were building to better his life – now had the job of getting me home. I had already created a mess behind me, and getting me to bed would limit any further damage. Georgie had willingly said I could stay at her house, which was 500 metres down the road from the bar I had just been ejected from.

At this point, the WhatsApp chats were going off.

Dom has done it again, x y z – everyone was made aware. The reaction, like it is to most people doing stupid stuff when drunk, was humour. Everyone laughed at the 23 year old doing stupid stuff. The normal reaction to my antics. But this wasn't normal.

Michael began shepherding me down the street. I refused, anger and ego came over me so I began not listening to him. I knew that getting to bed was the end of the drinking – Drunk Dom wasn't ready for that. It was 7.00 pm in summer, the sun was shining and I needed more fuel in me, the craving for more and more was growing. Largely because of the destruction I had caused, I wasn't drunk enough yet to forget that I didn't want to wake up in the morning to deal with this.

So, I resisted, falling into the road, nearly being hit by a car – a close call. I repeated this a number of times – there was a complete carelessness towards myself.

Michael took responsibility upon himself to see me home. Everyone else was in the position where they had 'washed their hands of me'. In my drunken state, Michael was the enemy. I couldn't see him for what he truly was – an excellent friend.

In taking me home, Michael was in the firing line and regrettably he was on the end of some vile abuse from me. In his own words, what I said led him into a 3-year-long crisis of confidence, which only intense therapy could repair. I knew I had caused him damage at the time, but it was only in my later years I realised how deeply those words cut. Despite the verbal abuse I hurled at him, he got me to Georgie's and got me to bed.

I had hurt one of my best friends, someone who was only trying to be there for me. Not only that, I had ruined my reputation. I believe in invisible PR – this is a force that either acts for, or against you. It is what people say when you aren't there. We all have invisible PR, although it's often a particular focus for others in business. A good friend of mine, Scott Thomas, shared that alcohol has impacted and damaged his personal life, like it had with mine. When it went into his business life, after getting escorted out of a club in front of his biggest client, it provided his wake-up call. For both of us in these situations there was no longer an upside to drinking, only destruction.

My PR had been destroyed. My destructive path had now caused major damage to someone I cared about. I had gone from a series of remote and near misses to a direct hit.

SCORING A DIRECT HIT

I often think about the role that fortune has played in my life, the monumental moments when being in a certain place, at a certain time, doing a certain thing, caused a knock-on effect with the rest of my life. Such moments include the story of creating a Twitter account and then dropping out of university due the social media page I'd created that I related in Chapter 1; my decision to go to France to watch Germany vs France, and even the patch of ice that I slipped on to break my ankle. The last two incidents are 'near misses'. To understand this phenomenon, consider the London Blitz of World War Two.

When Germany decided to launch a seemingly endless attack on London – 'the Blitz' – they wanted to lower the morale of the British people and bomb them into submission. Who would want to continue fighting a war in a foreign land when you lived through the sound of bombs hitting your neighbourhood and the streets you loved burning night and day? It is a sound theory – why would Brits risk London for the sake of a war in Europe?

What actually happened was a phenomenon called *Near Miss*. Malcolm Gladwell covered this in his book *David & Goliath*.

Gladwell explains (referencing psychiatrist J.T. MacCurdy) three things Londoners responded to during the Blitz:

1. people who were killed,
2. near misses, and
3. remote misses.

Here's what I want to dive into . . .

A **near miss** is a narrowly avoided collision or other accident. This results in trauma. These were the Londoners that were impacted by the bombs (possibly injured, but survived) and were traumatised by the experience. The result left the victims devastated.

A **remote miss** was when the Londoners (in Gladwell's example) heard the attacks and bombings, and may have been close to the destruction, but were energised rather than traumatised. In one example, he explains that a family elected to *not* flee London but to stay, excitedly saying something to the extent of . . . *What? Leave? And miss all of this?!* – referring to the excitement of the nearby bombings. Gladwell says, "A remote miss makes you think you are invincible." It can actually leave you stronger. Another word associated with a remote miss is invulnerability – the property of being incapable of being hurt (physically or emotionally). And, it is acquired courage.

The final two examples in Chapter 3 were remote misses for me. I had developed a sense of invincibility. Both of those days were incredibly stressful and in the moment immediately after each event I turned to alcohol to manage my emotion, thus strengthening the stimulus–response relationship between my emotions and alcohol. There was now an almost unbreakable bond between my emotions and alcohol. But they were not significant enough to lead to me feeling devastated or traumatised. They were not even near misses.

It wasn't until 23 July 2016 that I scored that direct hit. My drunken behaviour at the races, my awful behaviour with Georgie on the taxi ride back, my unforgivable behaviour in the bar and, finally, my appalling behaviour towards Michael, a friend trying to help limit the damage I had caused. The 23 July wasn't a remote miss or a near miss. This was a direct hit.

NOTES

1. Campaign against Living Miserably (2023). Suicide leading cause of death in men aged 20–49 in England & Wales. https://www.thecalmzone.net/onssuicidereport

2. *One in every 100 dies by their own hand, each suicide 'a tragedy'* – WHO. (2021, June 22). UN News. https://news.un.org/en/story/2021/06/1094212

3. Lisa Marzano, PhD, Dafni Katsampa, MSc, Jay-Marie Mackenzie, PhD, Ian Kruger, MSc, Nazli El-Gharbawi, MSc, Denika Ffolkes-St-Helene, Hafswa Mohiddin and Bob Fields, PhD (2021). Patterns and motivations for method choices in suicidal thoughts and behaviour: qualitative content analysis of a large online survey. https://www.ncbi.nlm.nih.gov/pmc/articles/PMC8058851/

4. *11 top health quotes to keep you going from Tony Robbins.* (2022, May 3). tonyrobbins.com. https://www.tonyrobbins.com/tony-robbins-quotes/health-quotes/

5. Lauren Geoffrion, MD (2023). How alcohol can impair judgement. American Addiction Centers. https://alcohol.org/health-effects/inhibitions/

6. Ashley Carucci (2022). What is all-or-nothing thinking and why it's important to manage it. PsychCentral. https://psychcentral.com/health/all-or-nothing-thinking-examples#all-or-nothing-distortion

CHAPTER 5

ROCK BOTTOM

The next day, I woke up. This felt different to previous times. There were too many witnesses, too many people had seen what happened. I didn't know if I could face Georgie or Michael. The tidal wave that had been building over the preceding months had come crashing down, leaving devastation in its wake.

This was the end of the line and end of the lies.

As an addict, the lies keep you safe. I had previously mastered no one seeing me and being able to insulate myself when I had become too drunk.

This time it was broad daylight.

My head was still spinning, and I was definitely still drunk. It was a Sunday morning. Sunday 24 July. The worst day of my life.

Even at this point, I hadn't made the connection that I or even alcohol was the major problem with myself.

But here I was, having just fallen through what I thought was another glass bottom, just a few weeks after the last incident where I broke my ankle, with the scars from the night before still fresh. The honest truth is, at the time I didn't know what I had really done, but the feeling of hangxiety or beer fear was consuming my thoughts.

It's the sinking feeling in the pit of your stomach and that rising sense of panic about what happened the night before that hits you at a time like this. There is good science behind why this happens. Tammy Richards',[1] who is a health practitioner, research shows this is due to a chemical imbalance in our body, which we have no control over.

GABA (gamma-aminobutyric acid) is the leading inhibitory neurotransmitter in the brain and is often related to relaxation – so when we drink alcohol, it binds to GABA receptors making us feel relaxed and chilled out.

Additionally, the amino acid glutamate contributes to beer fear. This is another chemical in the brain that plays an instrumental role in learning and memory. When we drink, our production of glutamate decreases and our GABA increases. As a result we feel more fearless, relaxed and confident, which is why alcohol is also called liquid confidence.

So, the morning after the night before, when our bodies start to break down the alcohol and it slowly leaves our system, our brain senses the chemical imbalance and tries to counteract it.

It does this by producing more glutamate and decreasing the amount of GABA, leading to our emotions being unbalanced. The sudden increase of glutamate is what sparks the fear and anxiety.

This mechanism derives from when we were required, early in our evolution as humans, to be in a constant state of survival mode. Anxiety, as a tool, helped humans survive for generations. The stressful stimuli that pushes our body into survival mode, and the activation of our stress-response system, focuses our mind on combating danger. In prehistoric times, these dangers were real. When *Homo sapiens* and our primate ancestors found themselves sheltering under lean-tos, in caves, and on branches they were relatively defenceless, and our ancestors faced the real possibility of being eaten by predators. Humans haven't always been top of the food chain and therefore our ancestors evolved many traits to help them escape that fate. Due to our comparatively slow rate of biological evolution these strategies are still within us and create the framework for how we live, even though as a society we have moved far beyond living in caves. When our ancestors heard, or saw, a sign of danger the hormones released would push us into a fight or flight response. When this happens, our heart rate increases, increasing blood flow to the muscles causing hyperventilation. This made us more likely to respond quickly to a predator to either fight it or give us the necessary physiological boost to run away and hide.

Today, these triggers still exist but no longer kick in only when we're faced with the real threat of being eaten. Instead, they can be activated by everyday activities – meetings, what we did last night, or just paying bills. The fight or flight responses don't really serve a purpose in these modern situations – other than making us more agitated.

That said, anxiety is not always a bad thing – it's designed to keep us safe, and I remember learning about positive anxiety when I was studying Sport Science. There's a spectrum and how far along it you fall at any given moment determines whether that anxiety is beneficial or detrimental. Anxiety tips into negative territory when it overloads us – such as when you have an anxiety attack and become unable to function or make decisions.

FACING MY BEER FEAR

On Sunday 24 July, my beer fear was real. I was still in bed when Steve messaged me saying he wanted to meet and talk about what happened the previous night.

The dreaded message that came through was short and to the point: "We need to talk." I knew this wasn't going to end well. I knew this was the end of the line.

My body responded, the chemical imbalance in my brain was already leading me to a state of shock, but the reality was that I was faced with those two primal options: run away or fight and face the danger head on.

At that moment, there was nowhere to run where I could hide. I felt like I was at the end of it all. The eternal sleep I had craved, the silence from the thoughts and feelings that had been running through my brain was no longer possible. It was a Sunday morning and running from the truth and from myself had to stop. Somewhere in the fog of my anxiety, I grasped that the wreckage I had created was one that couldn't be swept under the carpet, passed over as banter and overlooked again. This felt final.

As I got in my car to drive to meet Steve 45 minutes away, I was weighing up the options I had left. I was asking myself questions like: What am I fighting? Am I going to walk into this situation and blame everybody else? Can I lie myself out of this hole?

I felt like I was backed into a corner.

I saw no value in coming out swinging.

I felt the pressure and weight of my entire life on me. My friendships, relationship, business, all of them were slipping away as I was slipping away from my feelings.

As I walked into the office to speak to Steve, the gravitas of the situation was overcoming me. This was my life, a life I had contemplated ending due to the pain I was inflicting on myself, and up until that exact moment, all these thoughts were solely in my own head.

I had never expressed them to anyone. Keeping them under wraps was a battle that I was dreadfully losing, and that I was fighting alone. I was fighting every single day just to survive and get through it. It wasn't a way to be living and it wasn't a battle I could continue to fight for much longer. Just as Napoleon faced his Waterloo, this moment had undoubtedly become mine.

I turned the corner and saw Steve in the office. His face was one of disappointment blended with anger. A face can paint a thousand words and he didn't even need to say anything for me to read the situation.

All the strategies I had at my disposal played over in my mind. There weren't all that many. But the last one I came to as I saw his face was honesty.

When reflecting on the past few years of my life, the thousands of lies I had told myself and others, I realised that not once did I consider honesty would be the best policy – until I had run out of all other options.

Before Steve spoke any words, I just broke down in tears.

Through my emotional state I conveyed that I did not know what was going on with me. I felt I was breaking as a person. I didn't know why I was acting how I was. I was uncontrollable and when I added alcohol into the mix, it took control of me and turned me into someone else. All of this tumbled out of me and Steve listened.

Although the words we spoke that day may have been forgotten and as I was still in my hungover state my memory was pretty fragile for the following days – the one thing I will never forget is how his face changed. He talks about his experience in his first book *Happy, Sexy, Millionaire*, but from my perspective his face changed from one that was ready for war, ready for a battle to fight it out over the damage I had caused, to the face that I needed to see. A face that was staring into the soul of a broken man. Nothing came through him more than empathy and love. The vulnerable, damaged little Dom, who was using alcohol to mask all these feelings, finally found a forum to be able to talk to someone who was there, willing to listen, and willing to help. For the next few minutes this became the safest space in the world, in which my deepest, darkest, most destructive self-thoughts could be discussed with someone who not only shared some of those fears but wanted to help that vulnerable voice.

MEN WHO TALK...

For those moments, it felt like we were the only two young men in the world. Young men as a cohort of society can find it very difficult to talk about their emotions, and I was no different. Societal norms have created a social pressure that men need to be strong. As someone who's only experience in business prior to starting a company was that of seeing hard-faced Alan Sugar on *The Apprentice*, I believed that I had to be a central role model that everyone could turn to for support in their time of need, which is something that, as COO (chief operating officer) of the company, everyone constantly turned to me for. I wrongly perceived people expressing their problems as a sign of weakness, so there was no way that I was going to express mine. In some wider social constructs men who cry openly, or express emotions are considered weak. With my undertone of feeling like an imposter in my career for what we had achieved, my entire strategy had been to try to continue to display strength.

As I mentioned, in my experience those who could drink the most or drink the quickest were the strongest. These were real lads, Geordie Shore or Towie lads, the ones that always seemed to get the praise and accolades from others, and always seemed to have women flocking to them.

In addition, I was consumed with the fear of failure – failure of myself and the failure of the business, both of which I felt were the same thing. If the business fails, then I fail and vice versa. The closer I came to a perceived failure, the further I came from talking about it.

I had got to 23 years old and had no way of communicating how I actually felt – all the constructs that prevent men from speaking up about their feelings, abusive relationships, grief, fear of failure, and social pressure had led me to my rock bottom.

Biologically, my entire immune response was threatened. It was sensing real danger, feeling weak, mentally drained, broken and backed into a corner – I kicked into survival mode and in this darkest moment, I felt a level of strength I have never felt before.

I held my hands up, stopped the running and the lying and said "I'm not okay" and that "I needed help." These were words I'd never have spoken before that day. Call it pride, ego, or immaturity, the inability to effectively communicate my feelings had got me to the point where – if I didn't tell the truth – I know Steve would have suggested that I leave the company as the impact I was having had begun to significantly impact the business, the people within it, and our clients. I was at the end of the line.

As the conversation went on, I had to make a few promises. In the moment, I was still acting like an addict – I was there fighting for my own future and trying to limit the damage I had caused.

Steve told me I had to get help – neither of us really knew what that meant. Lisa, who was our PA at the time, had studied psychology, so her recommendation was to speak to a psychologist.

Now, my first thought was that psychologists were for crazy people – they were the white lab coat-wearing individuals from movies who put people in straitjackets to protect them from themselves. Of course I quickly learned how wrong that perception was, and in my situation, I had no position to negotiate – I had to sign up to the promises I needed to make.

So I agreed – the next day I was to see a psychologist.

The other promise I signed up to was to limit my drinking and even consider stopping. Again, I signed up and promised I would do that. Once again, I had no say in the matter so when I said it, did I really believe that I would never drink again?

Honestly, I don't think I did. Within me, I knew a slight realignment was needed, but to give up drinking, at the age of 23?

My first thought was . . . what would I even do on weekends?

I had discovered a narrow lens to view life through, the bottom of a glass of wine, and I couldn't see past that bottle to know that there was more to life. As I sat there with Steve that Sunday, I still held the belief that there wasn't anything more enjoyable than a few drinks; the drinks that numbed the pain I was feeling. If I got rid of that medicine, how would I be able to function and forget about all the pain I was in?

But, in the moment, the terms of my surrender to the situation were that I had to try these things.

I could tell Steve was at the breaking point of our partnership and he was tired of having to deal with me and the problems that I had created – but the topic that gave me the most belief in myself and our future was him opening up to the fact that, like me, he too had been struggling with all the pressure created by the plane we were flying and that it was having a major impact on him.

We had been best friends, business partners for a number of years, travelled the world together, and lived out of suitcases. We had enjoyed some of the greatest moments of our lives together and had built this business from our bedrooms into a major operation in a short space of time.

We lived together, and spoke every day, but not once in that time did we really open up about how it was making us feel.

Slowly, it had made us both sick – my problems manifested in a much more visible and destructive way than his, but he had his own battles. We shared the journey together, so of course our feelings would be similar, but it took a catastrophe for us to have the vulnerability to open up to each other.

Hearing that I wasn't alone and that he was having similar feelings around the anxiety, stress, and the problems we faced gave me reassurance that I wasn't weak, that I wasn't a failure for having these intrusive thoughts. Knowing this gave me hope that, actually, I could get through these issues but perhaps more importantly it also gave me a friend I could speak to about them. Someone who shared the same memories, foundations, and issues.

We sat next to each other for almost 3 years and neither of us knew how the other was really feeling until that day. We had both hidden from each other to try to protect ourselves. The only time we actually managed to protect one another was when we were honest.

I didn't know it at the time, but this was a really important part of my sobriety journey as it was the first step towards taking myself out of the emotional "box" I had closed myself off in. But I had a lot more work to do to rebuild the emotional connections in my life.

ESCAPING THE CYCLE OF DISHONESTY

This was when I began to break out of the cycle of dishonesty I had created within my life. I didn't realise then that the more lies I told, the easier it would be to keep lying.

When we engage in deceitful behaviour, our respiratory and heart rate increase, we can start to sweat and our mouth can go dry, but beyond the physiological signs, lying can also have a major long-term impact on our behaviour. A team of researchers at University College London and Duke University set out to find out what exactly goes on in the brain when we tell a lie.[2] In particular, they wanted to know whether the brain becomes desensitised to dishonesty over time, making it easier to tell a lie when we do so over and over again.

The researchers first had to prove that dishonesty increases over time. So they devised a task in which study participants could lie in order to receive money. To start, they presented participants with 30 pictures of glass jars, each containing between 1500 and 3500 pennies. The participants were asked to estimate, one at a time, how many pennies were in the jar. Then the participants sent advice (via a computer) to a partner whom they were told would submit an estimate on behalf of both of them.

Participants who made the initial estimate were told they would be paid according to how much their partner overestimated, while their partner on the other end of the computer would be paid according to how accurate his or her estimate was. As you may expect, participants faced the temptation to do something unethical: to lie about how many pennies they thought were in the jar so they could receive more money for themselves, even though it meant less money for their partner.

At first, participants lied only a little. They inflated their estimates by only a few hundred pennies. But over the course of the study, their inflated estimates became higher and higher. By the end of the study, their estimates were nearly twice as high as when they began.

In other words, dishonesty snowballed – lies started small but increased steadily in magnitude over time.

Early on, they saw a great deal of activity in regions of the brain associated with emotions – the amygdala in particular. This observation suggests that participants initially felt very bad about the lies they told. But over time, as participants lied again and again, these areas of the brain showed less and less activity.

My brain had become adapted to lying – when stimulus occurred I had started to lose the ability to feel bad about lying. The negative feelings no longer occurred, making it easier for me to continue to lie.

I had lied to Steve, my girlfriend, my parents, my family, and my team. But the lying and running had to stop. I had hurt some of the people I cared about most in my life. I couldn't look at my liver and see the damage I was doing internally, but I could see the pain in Georgie and Michael's eyes. I could see the hurt I was causing my family. Out of my love for all of them, I knew I needed to do something.

Did I believe myself when I said, "I'll never drink again"? I didn't. I was lying again. But now there were no more options. I was driven to change the cycle I had created.

NOTES

1. Naomi Jamieson (2022). 'The science behind beer fear'. https://www.myimperfectlife.com/news/beer-fear#:~:text=The%20amino%20acid%20glutamate%20also,decreases%2C%20and%20our%20GABA%20increases

2. Neil Garrett, Stephanie C. Lazzaro, Dan Ariely, and Tali Sharot (2016). The brain adapts to dishonesty. *Nature Neuroscience*, 19: 1727–1732. https://www.nature.com/articles/nn.4426

CHAPTER 6

CYCLE OF CHANGE

The next day, Monday 25 July 2016, after word had got out of what had happened a few days before, my stock had become low. My invisible PR, the things people say about you when you're not in the room, had become visible. I could see amongst colleagues and peers that they had no respect for me.

I managed through the day and Lisa had booked a session with a therapist for 7.00 pm that evening. I couldn't fail in my commitments to Steve and others at the first hurdle, so I willingly left the office and went. Pulling up outside a local supermarket in the middle of a normal looking housing estate – I could see a small door which said 'Office of Jamie Dempsay'.

As I sat in my £100,000 Mercedes AMG 63 car, which I had purchased a month earlier, intrusive thoughts started to come back to me, saying that I didn't need therapy, therapy is for weak people, what is this guy going to do for me? I sat in the car longer than I should have, contemplating the scenario where I did not go in – what would happen in that situation? Once again, the responsibility to others felt too great, so I popped open the door and rang the bell.

I remained open-minded to the possibilities of what this could bring for me. I reminded myself I needed help. But I was nervous – I had no idea what the etiquette was, what should I say or what should I do?

I walked up the stairs to be met by a smiling face. Jamie was no taller than 5' 6', wearing a crisp white shirt. He was a (I know he doesn't mind this) slightly overweight, bald individual with a softly spoken Scottish accent.

'God, how is he going to help me?' I said to myself.

He offered me a cup of tea, which he personally prepared for me and took me into his main treatment room. To my surprise the walls weren't covered in padding, nor were there clinical white lights or even a chaise lounge for me to lie on. This wasn't like the movies. This was just a front room, with two chairs facing each other and a glass table in the middle.

Jamie sat one side and I sat the other.

He had no context for who I was, what I was doing there or how he could help. So in my nervousness I explained everything to him – every little detail of how I was feeling, what my situation was and what issues I had caused.

There was no response from him.

So I carried on talking.

Jamie was a listener. Listening has so much power. As people we are all keen to talk, we enjoy the sound of our voices. But listening is a superpower.

In one laboratory experiment by Harvard Business Review[1] they assigned 112 undergraduate students to serve as either a speaker or a listener and paired them up, sitting face-to-face. They asked speakers to talk for 10 minutes about their attitudes toward a proposal for basic universal income or a possible requirement that all university students must also volunteer. They instructed the listeners to "listen as you listen when you are at your best". But they randomly distracted half of the listeners by sending them text messages and instructed them to answer these messages briefly (so the speakers saw that they were distracted). Afterwards they asked the speakers questions about whether they were worried about what their partner thought of them, whether they acquired any insight while talking, and whether they were confident in their beliefs.

They found that speakers paired with good listeners (versus those paired with distracted listeners) felt less anxious, more self-aware, and reported higher clarity about their attitudes on the topics. Speakers paired with undistracted listeners also reported wanting to *share* their attitude with other people more compared with speakers paired with distracted listeners.

Their findings suggest that being listened to makes an individual more relaxed, more self-aware of his or her strengths and weaknesses, and more willing to reflect in a non-defensive manner. This can make some more likely to cooperate (versus compete) with others, as they become more interested in sharing their attitudes, but not necessarily in trying to persuade others to adopt them, and makes them more open to considering other points of view.

Jamie was applying these principles to me. As with Steve the previous day, I had a safe environment, but the difference was there was no shared history, no prejudice, and Jamie was qualified to help. I had no reason to lie to Jamie, what was I trying to do? Impress him.

There were a number of things I said to him that day, which I had never openly said to anyone else. One of the few questions he asked me was, "Have you ever considered taking your own life?" to which I explained to him my fixation over train tracks and how I'd always thought "what if?".

Saying that out loud for the first time, I felt the gravitas of what I was saying. I was saying I do not want to be in this world anymore. Jamie gave little to no reaction to this. He remained silent while I continued talking.

As my tea started to cool and the end of the hour approached, I asked Jamie, "what is going on?" To which he explained clearly to me what was happening in my life as he saw it.

"Alcohol isn't your problem," he said.

My heart celebrated – thank god, I can carry on drinking.

"You are using alcohol as your coping mechanism, when things go wrong you instantly turn to alcohol to soothe the issue. In doing so, you're then not addressing the core issue and additionally creating more issues by your action. You have Alcohol Use Disorder (AUD)."

Like many, until this day I thought alcoholism was having vodka in the morning with your cereal, I wasn't aware there was a disease prior to this. The overview of AUD[2] is a pattern of alcohol use that involves problems controlling your drinking, being preoccupied with alcohol or continuing to use alcohol even when it causes problems. This disorder also involves having to drink more to get the same effect or having withdrawal symptoms when you rapidly decrease or stop drinking. AUD includes a level of drinking that's sometimes called alcoholism.

Unhealthy alcohol use includes any alcohol use that puts your health or safety at risk or causes other alcohol-related problems. It also includes binge drinking – a pattern of drinking where a male has five or more drinks within two hours or a female has at least four drinks within two hours. Binge drinking causes significant health and safety risks.

If your pattern of drinking results in repeated significant distress and problems functioning in your daily life, you likely have AUD. It can range from mild to severe. However, even a mild disorder can escalate and lead to serious problems, so early treatment is important.

The WHO has created a test you can do to see if you are someone who could suffer from AUD (see Figure 6.1).

Scoring:

§ 0 to 7 indicates low risk.
§ 8 to 15 indicates increasing risk.
§ 16 to 19 indicates higher risk.
§ 20 or more indicates possible dependence.

I scored 32.

After this diagnosis he slid me over a piece of paper titled 'The Cycle of Change'.

THE CYCLE OF CHANGE

Over the years, there have been many anecdotal conversations where I have ended up holding onto particular words

I'm Never Drinking Again

Alcohol use disorders identification test (AUDIT)

AUDIT is a comprehensive 10 question alcohol harm screening tool. It was developed by the World Health Organisation (WHO) and modified for use in the UK and has been used in a variety of health and social care settings.

Questions	Scoring system					Your score
	0	1	2	3	4	
How often do you have a drink containing alcohol?	Never	Monthly or less	2 to 4 times per month	2 to 3 times per week	4 times or more per week	
How many units of alcohol do you drink on a typical day when you are drinking?	0 to 2	3 to 4	5 to 6	7 to 9	10 or more	
How often have you had 6 or more units if female, or 8 or more if male, on a single occasion in the last year?	Never	Less than monthly	Monthly	Weekly	Daily or almost daily	
How often during the last year have you found that you were not able to stop drinking once you had started?	Never	Less than monthly	Monthly	Weekly	Daily or almost daily	
How often during the last year have you failed to do what was normally expected from you because of your drinking?	Never	Less than monthly	Monthly	Weekly	Daily or almost daily	
How often during the last year have you needed an alcoholic drink in the morning to get yourself going after a heavy drinking session?	Never	Less than monthly	Monthly	Weekly	Daily or almost daily	
How often during the last year have you had a feeling of guilt or remorse after drinking?	Never	Less than monthly	Monthly	Weekly	Daily or almost daily	
How often during the last year have you been unable to remember what happened the night before because you had been drinking?	Never	Less than monthly	Monthly	Weekly	Daily or almost daily	
Have you or somebody else been injured as a result of your drinking?	No		Yes, but not in the last year		Yes, during the last year	
Has a relative or friend, doctor or other health worker been concerned about your drinking or suggested that you cut down?	No		Yes, but not in the last year		Yes, during the last year	
Total AUDIT score						

Figure 6.1 AUD Test

Source: https://assets.publishing.service.gov.uk/government/uploads/system/uploads/attachment_data/file/1113175/Alcohol-use-disorders-identification-test-AUDIT_for-print.pdf

or phrases that were spoken during those conversations. Some of these conversations were with people I met once and have never spoken to again, others were with my nearest and dearest whose words had struck me so deep at a certain point that they became something I held on to.

As people we are generally not the best at taking advice from others. Geraldine Piorkowski studied this and published her results in *Psychology Today*.[3] The issue with taking advice from friends and family is that, as humans, we adapt to our surroundings, and not just our physical environment, but also our emotional one. We spend so much time with those closest to us that their advice or opinions blend into our thought process such that they become normalised to us. This works in the same way that seeing a beautiful view for the first time can be overwhelming and inspiring, but seeing that view for the 100th time diminishes how striking it was originally.

This effect of familiarity means that returning to the feeling you had when you first saw something is incredibly unlikely. This is why people want to discover new places and meet new people. That hit we get from doing something for the first time is always the greatest. A question I ask people in every interview I do is, "If you could watch one movie for the first time again, what would it be?" All respondents think deeply, going on an internal emotional journey to remember the feeling they had when a movie moved them so much that they want to recapture that feeling; but it is impossible to recreate that first-time experience.

Other reasons we don't really follow the advice, or even process the advice, of those around us is due to how difficult it is to override old perceptions of them. In my case, taking advice from people on my drinking issues, when I fully remember some of my friends getting into 'worse states' or 'situations' than I felt I was ever in, felt patronising. How can my peers, who are similar ages to me and still smashing alcohol themselves, be in a position to advise me what is right or wrong for me to do?

This leads to meaningful advice falling on deaf ears.

So, as I broke through glass bottoms and found myself on a downhill trajectory, the advice of those around me – who in truth were still doing the same thing I was being told not to – was always rejected. In my mind, there was a logical reason not to listen to them.

On that Monday after I hit rock bottom though, I found myself in a room with someone who had no preconceptions of me, nor did I have any long-term view on him. Someone who was intently listening to me – creating a safe space for me to talk about my feelings. Telling me the home truths that I had more than likely heard from those around me – but in honesty chose to reject.

I looked at the piece of paper he gave me on the Cycle of Change, shown in Figure 6.2.

I looked at it, reviewing each side of the cycle carefully and reflecting on my journey to see whether this was applicable to me at all. Despite finding the time I spent in this session useful, I was sceptical about the value of therapy, so naturally I was questioning everything. I looked at the stages in the Cycle of Change to try to pinpoint where I was currently.

Figure 6.2 Cycle of change
Source: Prochaska, J. O. & DiClemente, C. C. (1983). Stages and processes of self-change of smoking: toward an integrative model of change. *Journal of Consulting and Clinical Psychology*, Google Scholar.

Obviously I had just had a relapse, and had rapidly accelerated from pre-contemplation to action, by the fact I was sitting in my first therapy session. I had taken the first real step towards change.

Jamie then spoke about where most people fail on this journey.

He asked me where I thought the largest number of people failed. Given my experience, I quickly said "maintenance".

He glared into my eyes and said that no, in fact the most common area in which people get stuck in the cycle of change is the pre-contemplation stage. As humans, we don't change, we don't even contemplate the idea that we could change.

Tony Robbins, the world-renowned life coach and author said, "Change happens when the pain of staying the same is greater than the pain of change." I had heard this many times before but hadn't thought about the significance of it. At 23 years old I was used to adapting to and evolving my environment, moving to new places, exploring new countries. I never thought of the concept of change being about behaviour or my actions. As we get older and our behaviours become more ingrained in us, change becomes much more difficult.

I've looked into the most common reasons people are unable to make changes in their lives and also examined why, in my case, I was able to.

1. The current place is too comfy

As a species we are able to adapt to our environment and surroundings, so we quickly get comfortable with them and learn to live within our routine. We seek security and comfort at a really basic level. So effectively with a roof over our heads and a fridge full of food, a lot of our basic needs are met. In that situation, what is the point of breaking a habit or making a change to our life or career and seeking discomfort and making our life harder?

2. Consistency is key

A second reason a lot of people fail to make changes (and additionally the reason that I do not have a 'six-pack'), is they abandon their efforts too quickly as they expect immediate results. We've all experienced a new fad, especially in the form of 'diets' but constantly sticking to one of these and having the resilience to succeed is different.

We know that if we cut out pizza, cheese, fats etc., and add in vegetables, lean meat, and other high-quality proteins alongside managing portion quantities and mixing in an increase of movement of the body, there's a very high chance that we will lose weight, gain muscle, and tone up. Yet like most people I still find myself looking at takeaway menus on a Friday night for convenience and comfort. Some days I put the menu away, other days I order takeaway – I'm not consistent enough with my eating habits and therefore I haven't got a six-pack.

3. One change involves other changes

Specifically in relation to drinking, this is a major reason why change is difficult. To make a change in your life and stop drinking there are a lot of other parts of your life that also need to change. Throughout this book I have showcased how ingrained drinking is into our culture in the United Kingdom, how ingrained it was into my own personal life and how the comfort created from familiarity is a powerful draw for those struggling with alcohol.

To stop drinking, the adjacent changes you need to make can be as small as changing your weekly shopping order to as extreme as breaking friendships or moving to a facility or abroad.

So after going over the cycle of change with Jamie and him having just told me that I should give up drinking to focus on my mental wellbeing, I was left with a choice.

The result of this hour-long session could have gone one of two ways. I could genuinely learn from this relapse and begin an upward spiral of recovery by taking the advice of an individual who I'd only spent about an hour of my life with – I could mean it when I said I would not drink alcohol again or constantly repeat my bad behaviour. Or I could return to my self-destructive course and continue drinking.

My internal monologue, which was still going strong, was split into two thoughts. The first one was telling me that everything this man was saying was correct. That he was an expert and this was exactly what I needed to do.

The other part of my brain was telling me to tell him to shut up. Drunk Dom, although subdued without alcohol, was still in my head asking, how can I give up drinking? What does a 23 year old do on the weekends without going out? What is the point in life if I am going to miss out on all the great nights and experiences? I am going to be so boring.

Because this was a Monday, I knew I could at least do a few days of abstinence.

I made Jamie a promise that I would be back there at the same time next week – that I would not drink and that I would begin to think about the benefits of going through the cycle of change.

This was also the moment at which I began to realise that I was the problem. Having run out of excuses, I had reached a point where I had to hold my hands up and accept full responsibility. In doing so, I opened the doors to a period of self-improvement and this taught me a very valuable lesson – if I took responsibility, I also took control.

FACING MY TIDAL WAVE

My older brother always said that no matter what happened in my life, I always seemed to land on my feet. Until this point, he wasn't far wrong – I hadn't put much effort into my A-levels and had been given an offer to study at Edinburgh University; I'd dropped out of university to start a business that became incredibly successful. I was bouncing my way through life, and my brother resented me a little for that. He'd faced challenges along the way and been knocked back by them. I hadn't.

When I hit rock bottom, I think he thought I'd just bounce my way back. I didn't. I remember talking to him about this later, and describing what happened to me in July 2016 as being hit by a tidal wave – my feet were pulled out from under me, I didn't know which way was up and I was struggling to break the surface to breathe. I'd never been hit by a wave before so I didn't know how to swim. All my problems came crashing down on me at once, and I didn't have the coping mechanisms I needed to deal with them. That tidal wave ruined me for a time. If I'd been hit by a series of smaller, less damaging waves perhaps I'd have had the skills I needed to prevent a tidal wave from forming at all.

Your tidal wave could be anything – it is just a huge, scary problem that knocks you off your feet without giving you time to prepare or learn to swim. My point is that these tidal wave moments are extremely overwhelming, especially if you've had an easy ride until one hits you, like I had.

NOTES

1. Guy Itzchakov and Avraham N. (Avi) Kluger (2018). The power of listening in helping people change. *Harvard Business Review.* https://hbr.org/2018/05/the-power-of-listening-in-helping-people-change

2. Mayo Clinic (n.d.). Alcohol use disorder. https://www.mayoclinic.org/diseases-conditions/alcohol-use-disorder/symptoms-causes/syc-20369243

3. Geraldine K. Piorkowski, PhD (2022). Why is our advice to family and friends so often ignored? *Psychology Today*. https://www.psychologytoday.com/au/blog/beyond-pipe-dreams-and-platitudes/202209/why-is-our-advice-family-and-friends-so-often-ignored

CHAPTER 7

BREAKDOWNS TO BREAKTHROUGHS

I don't know who told me this, but it is one the best anecdotal lines anyone has ever said to me: breakdowns lead to breakthroughs.

This is the most salient phrase about sobriety I've ever come across.

As I mentioned earlier, I previously (and very mistakenly) had a perception that therapy was for those crazy types who are frequently seen in straitjackets. Clearly I had watched and believed too many Hollywood movies. By the time I had finished my first hour-long session, it's fair to say my perceptions of therapy had very much changed. I believed my entire life had been tossed upside down.

After promising Jamie that I'd stop drinking, my plans to go out for my friend's birthday at the weekend didn't seem like a reality I was going to achieve. I was well aware of the challenge, and the last part of my conversation with Jamie was me asking him bluntly – "How do I not drink, what do I do?"

It's only writing these words down today that I under-stand the level of honesty and vulnerability I showed in our session. But as someone who had now become a pretty good liar, actually being honest, not just with myself but with someone who was qualified to translate my problems into a diagnosis, was important.

This is an important message to anyone who is going through a difficult time at the moment, or knows some-one who is.

I think about that meeting with Jamie all the time: it's why now I am able to write this book after having achieved 7 years of sobriety.

I didn't realise it at the time, but I now believe deeply that the conversation I had with him saved my life. Call him a guardian angel, call it whatever you want.

There were so many sliding doors moments in my jour-ney but each one led me to walking into his room, exhausted, broken, and having nothing left to do but finally tell the raw, unvarnished truth of how I was feeling and what I was expe-riencing in my life.

Without my honesty I don't think I'd have been able to be fully diagnosed, nor would I have received his advice. A lack of honesty is a major problem I see particularly with men, but as I've said when you're addicted to anything your decision making around telling the truth can be com-promised. So my advice from my learning, honesty is the best policy.

My mission after walking out of Jamie's office was to create a strategy to be able to maintain the change of not drinking in my life and not relapse again. As Tony Robbins says, change happens when we are in pain, and I was in so much pain that I had to make this change in my life. I didn't believe in myself before, but after an hour with Jamie, I was starting to.

Alongside the cycle of change I reviewed the change equation:

$$D + V + F > R. \text{ [1]}$$

The model summarises Tony Robbins' view, as well as adding a couple of practical factors. Although what follows is applied to business context, I found it useful to translate to my own struggles.

D = Current levels of dissatisfaction

If dissatisfaction exists within the area where the change will take place the workforce will be far more motivated to support it. For example, an inefficient process of sending queries to senior managers will frustrate employees and the suggestion of a new system will gather support. Change initiatives can be success-ful even when employees are content with current sys-tems and processes, but generating support will be more difficult.

V = Shared vision of a better future

The proposition of a different future must be attrac-tive to all employees for a change to be successful, as they must see a benefit to their day-to-day activities. If the result of the change only appeals to a few employees, it will be difficult to generate enough support for it to be a success.

F = First steps in direction of new vision

The first steps of any initiative will be the most crucial. This is the opportunity to demonstrate the result of the change is not only desirable but also possible. The initiative must be carefully planned and communicated across the organisation to ensure everyone is on board with it. As the first few steps are taken, individuals will start to believe in it and support will grow.

R = Resistance to change

Unfortunately, resistance to change is inevitable as individuals become comfortable with their day-to-day processes, even if they are inefficient. Even if a change initiative aims to bring about a better process it is often hard to envision how this would work and employees are also unwilling to learn and adapt to a new process. Employee resistance is by far the largest barrier to change.

I've since reframed this to apply to my own situation at that time in 2016, just after my first therapy session with Jamie:

$$D+V+F>R. \text{[2]}$$

D = Current levels of dissatisfaction

The current level of dissatisfaction with my life and situation was very large. I was in desperate need of making this change in my life.

V = Shared vision of a better future

This was relatively low at this stage. I couldn't see what my life would look like without alcohol, and this was a potential risk. But I knew I had to make a decision on sharing this with others.

F = First steps in direction of new vision

These first steps for me involved taking in the advice of Jamie, and making the first few steps to achieve the vision.

R = Resistance to change

There was willingness to make a change, however dependency isn't straight forward and adding the levels of emotional turbulence in my life meant that one small change could derail any progress I made and lead to a relapse.

Please take this formula and apply it to any change you want to make in your life. Alongside these models, the advice Jamie left with me was:

To never be cold, hungry, or tired.

This dovetails with advice from Gateway Foundation[3] who use the acronym HALT – which stands for hungry, angry, lonely, and tired – as a strategy to avoid drinking in the first instance. The reason is that with most substances we become addicted to, including food or drink, we are driven by triggers. This could be the smell you get when you walk past a Subway sandwich shop or the need to grab a coffee as you walk past that same Starbucks every morning.

Triggers are also emotions, behaviours, or events that can cause you to crave drugs or alcohol. These triggers vary from person to person. Part of preventing relapse is recognising your individual triggers and putting strategies in place to help you deal with them. The following advice comes from the Gateway Foundation's website.

H: HUNGRY

There's a reason the term 'hangry' was coined. Hunger pangs bring out the worst in anyone, leading to intense emotions, irritability, and irrational decisions. When you don't have enough fuel to make good choices, you may settle on making a snap decision you'll regret. Try the following to ensure you never get caught off guard and hungry:

§ Carry healthy snacks such as fruit or granola bars.
§ Eat a hearty breakfast.
§ Make sure to stop for regular meals and snack breaks.
§ Don't snack on high-fat or high-sugar foods as these can drop your mood.

A: ANGRY

Getting angry from time to time is a part of being human. However, dwelling on situations or people that make you mad can lead to reckless decisions, such as returning to substance abuse. Prevent anger from getting out of control by:

§ Trying to understand what's causing your anger.
§ Finding a way to express anger that doesn't damage yourself or others.
§ Confronting situations that bother you head on.
§ Opening up about your anger instead of stuffing it down.

L: LONELY

You don't have to be alone to feel lonely. You can feel isolated when surrounded by people. That's why it's essential to have a support network of friends, family, and trusted individuals you can turn to when you feel tempted to use. If you're feeling lonely:

§ Call someone in your support network.

§ Attend a support meeting.

§ Shake up your routine and go where other people are.

§ Ask a friend to meet you for lunch or coffee.

T: TIRED

This may seem like the easiest trigger to address, but in our hectic culture, it's easy to get burnt out and exhausted. Lack of sleep is dangerous, though, as it impairs your ability to make good decisions, intensifies your emotions and makes functioning that much harder. These uncomfortable feelings can easily turn into a trigger to use drugs or alcohol.

Here are some ways to make sure you're getting enough sleep:

§ Go to bed early.

§ Try not to think about things that make you stressed or anxious right before bed.

§ Stop using electronics an hour or two before bed.

When looking at these resources and frameworks, I knew my potential weakness was (V) shared vision for the future. I had to find a way to achieve this because I didn't believe it within myself, but I knew it would be crucial for my recovery. Therefore, I had to find a way to generate that feeling and belief externally. So, I made the decision very early to go public about my decision to take a break from drinking with my friends, family, and colleagues. I openly told them it had started to impact my life negatively, which was why I was stopping.

This was almost like an intervention on myself. Within the first week after my first therapy session, I held serious, non-emotional conversations with those around me to tell them I was going to stop drinking.

While I knew that over the past few weeks my business partner and girlfriend had reached their limit with what they could take from me, it was something of a shock to learn they weren't the only ones. In the process of opening up, I spoke to other friends and family who all divulged to me that they were at the end of their patience with my actions. Constantly, I was ruining situations and occasions without a care in the world.

It was at this point when my own mother said, "We don't recognise you when you're drinking." This was another one of those anecdotal remarks that cut me like a knife. It wasn't one of those light slashes, but one which is stabbed right into your midriff, with the sheer force taking all the air out of you and finally twisting around to inflict maximum pain. Without my knowing it, these were my first steps on the process of the new vision.

First Steps

While normally, it is said the first step is the hardest, in my situation I found it the easiest, given that the pain and desire to change was so great. The difficult part was now maintaining it. When I was at school, in Year 8, our teacher asked us to write a letter to our future self. We were told to write down our aims, goals, and how we saw our life looking. At the time I was 12 years old, and I imagined what I would be doing at 18. On the last day of school, our English teacher gave us the letters we sent ourselves. I wrote about my dreams of playing football, who my friends were – it felt great seeing some of the things I aimed to do at 12 become a reality.

Our teacher used it to showcase the journey we went on at school and tried to capture a moment in time for eternity.

In my first week of stopping drinking, I decided to do the same. I decided to write a letter to my future self on the condition that it would be opened 2 years after achieving sobriety. I didn't know whether this would be in a 2 years' time, or longer (if a relapse occurred), but I knew I needed to capture how I felt at the moment.

Here is an extract from the letter:

My hope is that you've repaired all that was damaged and blossomed all that could flourish, because I'm sorry, I nearly destroyed your future.

By spending my first week openly repairing relationships and having honest and open conversations, not only did I start to rebuild my support network, but I created a ridiculously high level of accountability among those around me to attempt to achieve the goals I set around stopping drinking.

In a study published by the Professional Academy[4], it was shown that you are more likely to achieve your goal when you share it with someone – as long as that person is of higher status than you and/or you respect them.

Some productivity experts have also asserted that when you consciously decide you want to complete something you have a 20% chance of achievement. However, when you share your goal with someone the likelihood of success increases to 60%, and when you regularly 'check in' with someone the chances increase even further to 90%.

When the load is shared with those around you, then the 'check ins' become more frequent. So by opening up, being vulnerable and telling those around me about my ambition to remain sober, I shifted my odds from a 1-in-5 success rate to 9-in-10. Just as my drunken self had found safety in numbers to mask my drinking problem, my newly sober self now found safety in numbers to help me set out on a new path.

This is one of the greatest life hacks or pieces of advice I can leave with you – although it is difficult to be completely honest with the ones we love, sharing any difficulty in the long term is only beneficial. For context, I found it embarrassing, it was something I really didn't enjoy doing. It was tough having those conversations, and letting everyone around me know I was working to improve myself and change my behaviour.

The other thing that happened upon honestly sharing my situation was that I found myself in a position to receive advice. I had a genuine connection over a meaningful topic with many people during this time. In this roadshow of honesty, one of my friends recommended a book to me: *Chimp Paradox* by Professor Steven Peters.

Steve is a medical doctor; he specialises in mental health and the functioning of the human mind and has dedicated his working life to help people get the best out of themselves and to be in a good place. I was aware of who he was, given his previous work with Ronnie O'Sullivan, the greatest snooker player of all time. I had researched the work he did at university on performance and how to get the best mentality out of someone.

As not much of a reader, at this point in my life I had neglected all productive forms of self-development. As I was trying to find a way to fill my time that didn't involve alcohol, reading a book felt like a reasonable suggestion to occupy my mind.

This was the missing piece to my personal jigsaw of emotions and led to the most meaningful breakthrough I had experienced within myself.

Chimp Paradox[5] breaks down the brain into three segments:

§ The Chimp system – emotional, irrational, and survival based.
§ The Human system – rational, logical, and factual based.
§ The Computer system – our reference source.

These three parts of the brain work collectively in all our decisions. The chimp (fast acting) and the human (slow acting) are in constant conflict with each other and the chimp is trying to hijack your thoughts.

When the chimp takes control, we become emotional, reactive, and impulsive leading to an unhelpful internal environment.

This leads to things like negative self-talk, internalising and personalising feedback, being reactive to situations rather than responding correctly, living in chronic anger, and fear of anxiety.

This is what had happened to me in the few years leading up to my rock bottom in July 2016. My chimp was growing stronger, my chimp was that voice inside my head, my chimp had led me to make all those bad decisions.

While I feel having someone's 'chimp' or 'Drunk Dom' isn't taking responsibility for your actions, as part of the healing process you must always believe that there's a possibility you can become a better person. Of course, all the horrible things that happened were because of me, but I took comfort in knowing that it was caused by something that felt slightly separate to who I was deep down, and which at the time I didn't have any control over.

Alongside the advice I had received, stumbling upon Steven Peters' book exactly when I needed it contributed to me not only believing that I could reduce my (R) resistance to change, but it actually gave me meaningful practical steps to manage my chimp.

EXERCISE IT, BOX IT, FEED IT

Jamie, HALT, and Steven had all recommended food as a coping mechanism.

To stress, while a lot of what I've spoken about has come from my experience with drinking, there is a real possibility you could replace the term 'drinking' with any of the following: 'smoking', 'cheating', 'lying', 'betting', or even 'eating' etc. The triggers in our lives to which we are exposed can lead us to form any unhealthy habit, while the inability to form a positive change in our lives can stretch from not making our beds to major drug abuse. Understanding your **triggers** or **stimulus** and then understanding your **reaction** or **response** at a very basic level, alongside getting your head around the process of the cycle of change and finally the change equation, will see anyone make a major change to their life. The problem I faced was that I only started to learn these after crashing to my rock bottom when I was backed into a corner and forced to act upon it.

If I had learnt about this sooner, either through friends or family, or from my own research, I would possibly have been able to soften the blow and catch any potential problem before it became damaging.

This was my breakthrough and I see this as an opportunity for you, if you need help or know someone else who does. Take what I learned and have shared here and apply it to yourself or put it in front of whoever you know needs to hear it. If it wasn't for my breakdown, I would never have achieved the breakthrough. But with this knowledge hopefully you can soften the fall and catch yourself before you hit rock bottom like I did.

STORM BEFORE THE CALM

The first weekend of not drinking was the toughest. I walked into our office on Friday and decided I was going to return home to see my family. I knew I would find no comfort or limited support around a group of 20-somethings looking to blow off steam at the end of a long week in an office that had a bar. As I embarked on the 2-hour drive home, the first question which entered my mind was:

When was the last time I didn't drink an alcoholic drink?

Challenging myself to remember the longest I had gone without a drink was difficult. I racked my brain looking back at all the things I had done over the past few years and I was genuinely shocked at how hard this was to try to recall. The best guess I could manage was to estimate that it had been no longer than 3 or 4 days between drinks after I was packed off to university at 18 years old.

So, given that this was day six of my dry spell, I mentally congratulated myself for going the longest I believe I had ever had without drinking alcohol since I was legally allowed to do so. Having an ability to pause and stop, to self-reflect, served as a real insight.

I then Googled: 'What happens to your body when you stop drinking?' and stumbled upon the Delamere blog. The following are direct extracts from what I read:[6]

3–7 days: Withdrawal symptoms will, on the whole, stop for most people. In a few cases, the symptoms will worsen and can develop into the medical emergency delirium tremens (DTs), involving disorientation, confusion, and profuse sweating. Heavy use can lead to alcohol lasting up to 3 days in your body.

I also scrolled down to read:

1 Year: A few people will find [that] some degree of the sense of low energy, anxiety, sleeping troubles, and/or alcohol cravings present at the beginning of withdrawal continues for much longer than is usual.

At the 12-month mark, almost everyone will leave these behind and begin to enjoy all the benefits of being drink free.

On one hand, I thought that I'd never given my body the chance to recover and remove alcohol completely from my system, and on the other hand I became aware I had up to a year to wait to realise the true benefits. That night I had a grounding time with my family and for the first time on a Friday night for a very long time, I took myself to bed – after giving myself a rewarding meal, for achieving the longest I ever had gone without drink – sober.

The next morning, I woke up and. . . felt as bad as if I had been drinking. There was no early morning feeling of being fresh on a Saturday morning. I woke up reaching for my water, dehydrated with a headache and stiff limbs. This feeling wasn't new, this felt just like a hangover. I started saying to myself that there's no value in sobriety, it feels exactly the same as drinking just without the fun of going out. I questioned everything, from the food I ate last night, to whether I had accidently had a drink. Is this just what sobriety is like? It wasn't what I'd expected.

I described what I had as a 'phantom hangover' to my parents.

It turns out I wasn't the first person to experience one.

Simply put, a phantom hangover[7] is your body creating the normal symptoms of a hangover when you haven't had any alcohol. A few days, weeks, or even months after quitting alcohol you may be surprised and dismayed to wake up with the old familiar feeling of a hangover. The symptoms may be psychosomatic, or side effects of chemical imbalances resulting from suddenly stopping frequent alcohol use.

Here I was, having taken every possible step to improve my life, only to find myself once again feeling like shit trying to get out of bed on a Saturday morning. This isn't the best advertising campaign for sobriety. But I've spoken already about the need to be honest, and there's no point in hiding the fact that, at the start, sobriety can feel no better than drinking. You just have to get through it.

Over the first few months, I experienced a number of phantom hangovers – all coinciding with a 'first'. My first night out again, my first festival, and as I've just shared, my first Friday night – this could put you off changing your relationship with alcohol but, it shouldn't. Here is what I would do to combat a phantom hangover.

AFTER QUITTING ALCOHOL IT'S OKAY TO INDULGE A LITTLE IN LESSER VICES

First and foremost, it's important to realise that it's okay to prioritise quitting alcohol over many other aspects of keeping a healthy lifestyle during the early stages of quitting.

If you wake up with a phantom hangover and are feeling awful, maybe indulge in an extra hearty breakfast, or don't feel guilty about getting a donut if it'll give you a quick cheap endorphin rush to get your brain back on the right track for the rest of the day. Don't feel bad about napping and being lazy all day if that's what you need. Take a day off work to do nothing if you can manage to do so without damaging your career. If that's not an option, get an extra coffee in the afternoon if you need an energy boost. Remember, these are quick fixes, and be careful not to form any new permanent bad habits. But during the early stages of sobriety your main focus should be abstaining from alcohol and it's okay to not be saintly in all areas of life. Once the psychosomatic symptoms start to subside, you should start to focus heavily on shifting to an all-around healthy lifestyle.

I had to make removing alcohol from my life my number one priority. This comes at the sacrifice of other areas of your life. The first two areas I saw major life changes in were my 'friends' and my diet.

My relationship with alcohol was largely emotional. What I would find was that if I had a bad day, in my personal life or at work – I would drink.

The same would happen if I had a good day, I would drink.

This ultimately built a stimulus and response connection between my emotions and my brain's urge for alcohol (see Figure 7.1).

While this might sound rather basic, forming a relationship with alcohol in this way can be scary.

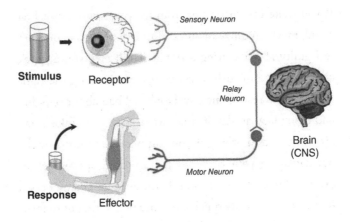

Figure 7.1 Stimulus response model
Source: https://ib.bioninja.com.au/standard-level/topic-6-human-phy-siology/65-neurons-and-synapses/stimulus-response.html

A stimulus is anything that causes you to react, for example, the smell of food. Responses are actions of the body: muscle contractions, gland secretions, or brain action.

I remember thinking to myself, if my connection with alcohol is now this deep, in that my body is physically expecting a binge drinking session on my first weekend of not drinking, I am in a serious state. This means that on a biological level, my body has already changed. I was intent on understanding the biology behind this. Why had I experienced a phantom hangover?

After reading about the stimulus response model I understood that, given that I had experienced a phantom hangover, it was very likely that my requirement for alcohol had embedded into my central nervous system (CNS). This meant that at a motor neuron level my body had chosen to respond involuntarily, because there was no external stimuli (alcohol). It had just predicted that it would need to respond, based on the fact that I usually consumed large quantities of alcohol. When I really sat down and thought about what I was putting my body through, it scared me.

Edward Thorndike (1874–1949), a US psychologist, developed a theory of connectionism. He proposed that learning happens through making attachments through stimuli and responses.

Think back to secondary school when learning about Pavlov's dogs, and how he managed to train the dogs to drool at the sound of the bell, because they were anticipating the food to come. This led to Thorndike creating the three elements that make up the law of learning, which explains that for every stimulus in your life, you learn a response. Those responses are influenced by effect, readiness and exercise.

The law of learning works for every stimulus and response. It states that repetition strengthens the connection between a stimulus and a response. Thorndike proposed that the nature of the S–R connection could change and become stronger or weaker. Successive connections between a stimulus and response make the connection stronger.[8]

There are three parts to the law of learning:

§ the law of effect,
§ the law of readiness, and
§ the law of exercise.

LAW OF EFFECT
This effectively means that when a response is accompanied by a rewarding effect, in a given circumstance, there is an

increased chance of the response being repeated in the same circumstance.

So, in relation to drinking, I had built up a number of strong rewarding occasions when I actually felt alcohol had enhanced my life. I'd had a number of enjoyable nights out, parties, and evenings with friends when alcohol was around, but no damage was caused.

I'd also had nights where alcohol was the best medicine, where I went out, and forgot all my problems for that night. In the moment, I had some very enjoyable occasions, that is true. But in my decline through that emotional connection, I had ultimately formed a strong association with alcohol as a coping mechanism.

LAW OF READINESS

This law states that learning is dependent upon the learner's readiness to act, which facilitates the strengthening of the bond between stimulus and response. Thus, an athlete who is highly motivated and eager to learn is more likely to be receptive to learning than one who is poorly motivated.

LAW OF EXERCISE

Connections become strengthened with practice. For example, the more an NBA player practises, the better they get.

I had been strengthening the connection between alcohol and my emotions by drinking every day. This explained how a downhill spiral could occur. What potentially started out as a drink in my hotel room after a terror attack in Paris, causing my first real panic attack – evolved into drinking every day to manage daily emotions. There was a continuous exercising of the connection, which now had forged a solid relationship.

It made sense to me. That my urge for alcohol had gone down to a neuron level and was wired into my central nervous system showed I needed to do something about it.

The model is simple: Stimulus = Response

There are only two things you can influence. Either you can try to change the stimuli, or you can adapt and evolve your response.

I was running a fast-growing company. The reality was that all my negative stimuli were coming from the business. There was the uncertainty over cashflow, the imposter syndrome of feeling like a fraud running this company, and the day-to-day general stress that comes with a position of responsibility.

On top of that, I had now started to hate myself, particularly how I looked, my eyes had become puffy, my hair had started to fall out – and at the tender age of 23 that is mortifying. I had begun to lose friendships and was on the edge of losing another relationship. I had burnt all my bridges and opportunities.

This made me think – and these were my personal darkest thoughts – that life would be easier if I chose to remove all those stimuli from my life. If I was to walk away from the company, and either get myself healthy or just to get away from everything that was going on, life would just be easier.

For a few days I considered these options, as deep down I felt that walking away from the business was a more realistic option for me as it would mean I would be able to drink again – and to be 'normal'.

Now, I can imagine how that sounds. I was willing to walk away from one of the UK's more exciting young companies and a life I never could have imagined before, all for the ability to drink again one day. It doesn't sound like a rational mindset. I'm not going to pretend that it was. But it's where my head was at in those early days of my sobriety.

DISNEY DREAMER

It was during one of these days at home, I looked at a picture on my wall. One of my friends had given me a picture of a quote from Walt Disney after I started Social Chain. It was probably one of the most meaningful gifts any friend has given me. Disney is my favourite brand and the story of Walt Disney's journey and his creativity has always inspired me.

The quote is:

> I only hope that we never lose sight of one thing . . .
> That it was all started with a mouse
> Walt Disney

My friends had constantly joked with me that my entire business had all started with a Tweet. So the quote by Disney really struck home with me in this situation, for two reasons.

First, it acted as an inspiration for remaining on the journey that I was on, and that incredible things can happen with just the humblest start. But secondly it also made me think of Disney stars and other young celebrities of my generation.

Many famous people such as Lindsay Lohan, Brittney Spears, Demi Lovato, Justin Bieber, Macaulay Culkin, and Jake Lloyd have experienced 'success' at a young age and gone on to have their lives ripped apart by addiction driven by fame. Although I had in no way achieved anything like they had, I felt a certain similarity to them. After all, I had all the means to be free: a nice house, a £100,000 car, the expensive watches, and while I wasn't exactly walking in their shoes, I had managed to have a glimpse of what that life can be like: New York VIP festivals and penthouses. It was enough of a sample to feel familiar with their situations. So at that moment, it might seem strange to say, I didn't feel alone.

In researching the topic of celebrities and alcoholism, I also stumbled upon celebrities who were sober. The list shocked me to my core. Among them were Bradley Cooper, Brad Pitt, and Gerard Butler. These were some of the biggest names in Hollywood, genuine idols of mine whose movies I'd deeply enjoyed. Each of them had a similar story of how alcohol had ruined their lives and now they are happier than ever sober.

When I was 21 years old I thought the only way to be successful through culture, media, or advertising was to spend loads of money, drink loads of alcohol, and buy designer clothes. I was led to believe through the influences around me that that's just what you did.

To now learn that there were some men who I already deeply respected who hadn't followed that path made me think again. The more I researched their sobriety stories, the more it filled me with hope.

It was also one of the most defining moments in my relationship with my partner. My now father-in-law, Jim, is a cousin of Gerard Butler. They spent a lot of time together when younger and in fact Jim told him he needed to sort himself out. This was prior to his acting career. At the time Jim had this conversation with Gerard, he was a lawyer. Having this first-hand experience, in my partner's family, resulted in what I believe was my second (and last) chance and showed me definitively that the route of sobriety was possible with an incredible individual who went on to global recognition within his industry as a role model.

At this point I realised that walking away from the business would be crazy. I had more to give there and therefore I ruled out removing the stimulus for my drinking – aka my stress at work. I arrived at this decision based on the same principles I followed when I dropped out of university, that is to say, because I had clarity provided by the information about why I was drinking, I also had a delusional belief that I could beat it without doing the work. That I could conquer it and that no challenge was too big for me. That confidence in my abilities had the potential to be positive, but not when it was supported by the delusional belief that I didn't have to put in the hard work to achieve my goal of beating my alcohol addiction.

What's more, due to my insecurities I had spent years portraying a sense of self-belief to others when the reality was that it was fake. Having had the tidal wave break over me and wash away those fake assertions that I believed in myself, I needed to build up genuine self-belief.

Self-belief is a skill, and like all skills they can be taught. They just need to be practised. You can learn the skills needed for securing mini wins in your life, which can build confidence. Practice can be as simple as improving your public speaking skills by talking in front of two people, then building on that over time until you are speaking in front of over 50 people. The positive reinforcement of completing each task gives you more self-belief that the next time you face the same situation, you will succeed.

To stop drinking, I needed to build up my self-belief that I could, and that meant I had to change my internal narrative. Instead of telling myself I needed to drink, I had to find a way to shift my perspective and tell myself that I could go sober, even though I had no previous experience to support that in my adult life. But what I did have was experience of having overcome a deep-rooted self-belief about running.

In secondary school I had a few glaringly obvious weaknesses that are revealed when looking at my school reports and achievements. My first weakness was that, despite being technically capable at sports, I detested cross-country (long-distance) running. I wasn't very good at it. I remember in the Year 9 house competition sprinting the first 200 metres, shouting "I'm first" only for the rest of the year to pass me one by one.

In fact I was one of the worst in the year. I detested it so much that in Year 10 when the cross-country distance doubled in length I asked my Dad (who is a GP) to help me come up with an injury that would mean that I wouldn't be able to do cross-country in PE on a Tuesday but would still be able to play football on a Wednesday.

Despite him frequently telling me no – he eventually helped me with a diagnosis of Plantar fasciitis – a repeated strain injury of your heel that became inflamed with the beating on the road during cross-country but would be fine for me to play football the next day.

Because I was on the football, basketball, and cricket teams, I was viewed in a slightly different light to others that attempted to dodge cross-country. I almost feel that Andy Bell, my all-time favourite teacher and head of PE at my school, knew what I was doing and let me get away with it. From this, there came a running joke amongst my peers that I would sell my soul to avoid cross-country. I just hated running. Or that was what I told myself.

I felt like I had always carried this story with me – we'd still joke about it between friends. When I was 19 I wanted to try to change the narrative and people's views of me. So I went for the ultimate conquest. I decided I was going to run a marathon.

On 20 October 2013 I completed the Yorkshire Marathon in just over 4 hours. No one around me believed it. I had taken what was my biggest weakness and effectively achieved the Everest of that. This required dedication, sacrifice and self-belief. Every single data point I had experienced in my life so far told me that I was not going to enjoy this, I wouldn't achieve it, and that life would be easier if I didn't.

Little did I know that running a marathon at 19 to change people's perspectives of me and to challenge my own self-beliefs would prove to be a crucial mental tool in my fight against addiction. Knowing that I had changed a self-belief in the past certainly helped me as I worked to change my internal dialogue around alcohol. I took the principle that I could change my weaknesses into strengths, and applied this to my sober journey.

The route to an easy life isn't to take easy decisions or choices, the route to an easy life is to make tough choices.

The tough choice I made was to stay at the company, to try to adapt my response to the stimulus that I was experiencing. It felt difficult, walking back into an environment that wasn't going to change and where I was the one who needed to make the changes.

I can see the appeal of a rehab facility, where your single focus can be on recovery and healing yourself. Taking you away from friends, influences, difficult situations, and effectively wrapping you up in cotton wool so that the Stimulus–Response connection just weakens over time as it isn't exercised.

But rehab wasn't an option for me. I decided I needed to first pick a new response and alongside that, work on reducing the impact the stimulus was having on my life.

THE NEXT ADDICTION

The new response I chose, effectively becoming my next addiction, was food.

Remember that addiction is a disease and not just a bad habit. What I was unwittingly experiencing was addiction replacement,[9] also known as addiction substitution or transfer addiction. This happens when an individual in recovery or rehabilitation replaces one addiction with another. The aspect here, which was important for my situation, was that the stimulus and underlying issues, such as my anxiety and imposter syndrome, and psychological needs that were driving my addictive behaviour in the first instance weren't going to be solved quickly – so with my decision to effectively 'carry on as normal' this was an essential survival strategy for me.

I was still trying to fill the psychological void. I knew in my recovery I was going to address the negative feelings and problems in my life, but for that I needed time. To give myself that time, I needed something else to help manage my emotions and get me through the day. In researching this area, I always found that the desires for fatty food and alcohol share the same chemical trigger.

Alcohol produces galanin, which in turn promotes the consumption of alcohol. This is why alcohol is addictive, your body craves more of it. A research paper by Steven Schultz[10] based on a study during which rats were injected with galanin, a natural signalling agent in the brain, found that the rats would drink increasing quantities of alcohol even while consuming the normal amount of food.

Galanin, a kind of small protein fragment, had previously been shown to play a role in appetite, particularly for fatty foods. The consumption of fat causes a part of the brain called the hypothalamus to produce more galanin, which in turn increases the appetite for fat. In healthy people there are counteracting signals that break this loop.

This felt like this was the explanation I was looking for.

Alongside this I looked into the relationship between alcohol and dopamine and food and dopamine: alcohol has a powerful effect on dopamine activity in the brain. When we drink, the brain's so-called reward circuits are flooded with dopamine. This produces euphoric feelings – or what we recognise as feeling 'buzzed'. Dopamine[11] also activates memory circuits in other parts of the brain that remember this pleasant experience and leave you thirsting for more. But over time, alcohol can cause dopamine levels to plummet, leaving you feeling miserable and desiring more alcohol to feel better. Certain foods, particularly those rich in sugars and fat, are potent rewards that promote eating (even in the absence of an energetic requirement) and trigger learned associations between the stimulus and the reward (conditioning).

This felt like it was it, like my own personal cheat codes. Alcohol and food lead to the same chemical and emotional reaction in your body. Now, like most people I don't fully understand the science behind this, but the simple equation made me believe that I would be able to identify when I was feeling triggered, and understand that my chimp wanted me to react immediately. But now I would be able to understand and process my response in a healthy manner.

So I began on the journey that Dr Steve Peters and Jamie had recommended. From Jamie I gained the awareness of what was going on with my mental health and how I was acting. Alongside that was the learning I had begun to do myself, particularly those from Dr Steve Peters' book. I had made several breakthroughs; and my survival mode was activated.

NOTES

1. Richard Beckhard and Reuben T. Harris (1987). *Organizational Transitions*. Reading, MA: Addison-Wesley Pub. Co.
2. Richard Beckhard and Reuben T. Harris (1987). *Organizational Transitions*. Reading, MA: Addison-Wesley Pub. Co.
3. Gateway Foundation (2023). Dangers of HALT. https://www.gatewayfoundation.org/addiction-blog/halt-addiction-recovery/#:~:text=HALT%20%E2%80%94%20hungry%2C%20angry%2C%20lonely,triggers%20that%20lead%20to%20relapse
4. Kat Knights (n.d.). Accountability: The key to achieving your goals. Professional Academy. https://www.professionalacademy.com/blogs/accountability-the-key-to-achieving-your-goals/#:~:text=What%20is%20the%20importance%20of,and%20%2F%20or%20you%20respect%20them
5. Peters, S. (2012). *The chimp paradox: The Acclaimed Mind Management Programme to Help You Achieve Success, Confidence and Happiness*. Random House.
6. Alex Molyneux (2020). A timeline of what happens when you quit drinking for good. Delamere. https://delamere.com/blog/a-timeline-of-what-happens-when-you-quit-drinking-for-good
7. StopDrinkingAlcohol.com (n.d.). What is a phantom hangover? https://stopdrinkingalcohol.com/what-is-a-phantom-hangover/

8. Kelly Carroll and Natalie Boyd (updated 2023). Connectionism definition & laws. https://study.com/ learn/lesson/connectionism-laws-philosophy-impact-edward-thorndikes-theory.html#:~:text=The%20 law%20of%20exercise%20states,response%20 make%20the%20connection%20stronger

9. Gateway Foundation (2023). Substituting one addiction for another. https://www.gatewayfoundation.org/ addiction-blog/substitute-addictions/

10. Princeton University (2004). Desires for fatty foods and alcohol share a chemical trigger. http://pr.princeton .edu/news/04/q4/1215-galanin.html

11. Amy Keller (2023). Alcohol and dopamine. Drug Rehab.com. https://www.drugrehab.com/addiction/ alcohol/alcoholism/alcohol-and-dopamine/#:~:text= Alcohol%20causes%20the%20brain's%20reward, groundwork%20for%20an%20alcohol%20addiction

CHAPTER 8

ROAD TO REDEMPTION

As part of this journey, I have kept photos and a timeline of events that I attended over the following few months. When I started out, unwillingly with Jamie but taking his advice to stop drinking, I set myself a target. Goals need to be realistic and need to be measured. As a result of how habitual my drinking had become there was no way I could have walked out of the first session with Jamie and I said "I am never drinking again."

The first challenge was to not drink for 3 months. I thought that would be long enough for me to be able to reintroduce alcohol into my life. I could take a short break out of my life, rest, charge up, and figure out all the problems I had and be enjoying Vin Chaud and mulled wines by Christmas. My self-belief was acting a little bit too strongly at that point – however very quickly the 3 months extended to 6 months, I was going to get to Christmas without having a drink. In my mind I would celebrate by pouring myself a special bottle of red wine – the last one I had in stock from the 48 our investor got us for winning the 'Best Agency Award' in April 2016.

That became my goal, and I told everyone so that I was accountable not just to myself, but to all of those around me as well. I also booked in a weekly session with Jamie, Mondays at 7.30 pm.

The weekdays were easier than the weekends. I had my purpose. I was just throwing myself entirely into work. I knew that I had avoided problems professionally for too long. There was no more running away from my problems, these things needed to be addressed. I was determined to hit my goal now that I had a real second chance. This business was going to be something special. At the time we had potential, but I knew it could have been something more.

In start-up culture, everything can be a little bit manic at times, especially when the business is growing so quickly. I had no previous professional experience but found it easy to remember things. This was great for running a business when there were between 5 and 10 of us, but when the company grew, not only did scaling too fast lead to mistakes and things being forgotten – it was entirely inefficient and was making the business unstable.

In the early days of recovery, my attitude was to listen to advice and I was ultimately willing to try anything. I had a completely open mind for whatever could lead to improvement in my life. One recommendation Jamie came up with was journaling.

JOURNALING

The University of Rochester's Health Encyclopaedia website says this about journaling:[1]

Journaling helps control your symptoms and improve your mood by:

- *Helping you prioritise problems, fears, and concerns.*
- *Tracking any symptoms day-to-day so that you can recognise triggers and learn ways to better control them.*

I had to prepare a journal of my week but writing down each day how I felt, any specific triggers I had noticed, and any tasks that I had to do that were unfinished.

It was effectively my homework. I would bring it to sessions each Monday and during the first 10 minutes we would go over the journal to discuss anything that might be significant. The process of transitioning thoughts in my mind into words on paper that were going to be discussed felt revolutionary. It felt like I was freeing up space in my mind. The journaling evolved into a daily diary of things I had to do in the office, a to-do list. I had never previously tracked my tasks and found the completion of my list and journal empowering for what I was going through.

BENEFITS OF JOURNALING

WebMD describes the benefits of journaling like this:[2]

It can reduce your anxiety. Journaling about your feelings is linked to decreased mental distress. In a study, researchers found that those with various medical conditions and anxiety who wrote online for 15 minutes three days a week over a 12-week period had increased feelings of well-being and fewer depressive symptoms after one month. Their mental

well-being continued to improve during the 12 weeks of
journaling.

It helps with brooding. Writing about an emotional event can
help you break away from the nonstop cycle of obsessively
thinking and brooding over what happened – but the timing
matters. Some studies show that writing about a traumatic
event immediately after it happens may actually make you
feel worse.

It creates awareness. Writing down your feelings about a difficult situation can help you understand it better. The act of
putting an experience into words and structure allows you to
form new perceptions about events.

It regulates emotions. Brain scans of people who wrote about
their feelings showed that they were able to control their emotions better than those who wrote about a neutral experience. This study also found that writing about feelings in an
abstract way was more calming than writing vividly.

It encourages opening up. Writing privately about a stressful
event could encourage some to reach out for social support.
This can help with emotional healing.

Journaling is so powerful when done correctly. When
combined with a review session with an expert, it felt like it
unlocked all the potential possible.

HAPPY BABY

The second tactic was to run hard towards friends, family
and loved ones. While the week had been taken care of with
work, surrounded by people, always able to occupy my mind

and thoughts – the weekends were much more difficult to navigate. I learned that first weekend that avoidance – my only strategy at the beginning – was soon not going to be effective. I needed to build something a bit more robust and sustainable since my first thought was 'what am I going to do now, that I don't drink?'

I remember in one of our later sessions telling Jamie this. We began to discuss the concept of 'happy baby', which is similar to the concept of your 'inner child'. When drinking, I had lost any sense of who I was, what I valued, and what I enjoyed doing. Given alcohol is only legal after the age of 18 in the United Kingdom, there had been plenty of happy times in my life without drink. My entire personality wasn't determined by alcohol. I knew I needed to reconnect with what I used to enjoy.

Reconnecting with your inner child[3] has been shown to improve health and your sense of well-being. It can restore joy to your life and help you find purpose. The concept is based on four pillars of gaining useful life lessons through childhood experiences. These pillars are: sharing relationships, playing to heal, being strong or frail, and supporting the next generation. I had lost my sense of myself, between work and drinking I had neglected quality time with friends. Every occasion was about drinking – instigated by myself mostly, but sometimes by others. We'd meet at Bottomless Brunch at 12.00 pm, have our first drink by 12.01 pm and would be stumbling off on our own by 10.00 pm. Where is the quality in that?

There were no meaningful conversations, there were no deep emotional chats, there was little difference from one night to another. Some of the stories last to this day, they are shared experiences we all laughed and joked about. As we matured, we needed more from our friendship. As I explain later in this chapter, men especially need friends around them who can check in on them, friends who they can open up with about difficulties they are facing. It's not that women don't need this, it's just that they are generally better at doing it. In my experience, this is something men struggle with though. Being seven pints down by 3.00 pm on a Saturday afternoon most weekends wasn't leading to strong meaningful connections.

As children we used to spend all day kicking a football at a wall, playing ridiculous made up games with any stones and targets we could find or simply riding our bikes to the park – there was life before alcohol and I needed to learn to remember what that was like.

One of the best decisions my friends and I made when I was starting my recovery, was to all go away as friends to Centre Parcs. It was roughly 6 weeks after I had stopped drinking and a weekend spent playing sports, going on the rapids, and not centred around alcohol started to shift my view on what was possible. Not only had I got friends supporting me – not doing the "just have a drink" or my personal favourite "don't be boring," these were people who were going to support me through this process – but I started to reconnect with things I enjoyed doing. There was a sense of joy in my life that I had not experienced before.

Despite my inability to stay up past 9.00 pm either day of the weekend, with mental and emotional fatigue frequently hitting me, I not only survived, I thrived.

Next was my family. Throughout the turmoil of my life, I felt significantly that I had let them down. One example of letting them down before my sobriety was being open with my mother about my substance abuse, at 3.00 am, with my arms flailing around like I was drowning in a swimming pool, after one of my friends had managed to get me home. At this time, I needed them, I needed some stability and grounding. I'm thankful that despite my actions I was welcomed back home, that they never lost hope. They were always going to be there for me.

I remember fondly a night that I shared with Jamie in my journal as the highlight of my week. It may sound ridiculous, but I got home on a Friday evening and my mum had bought a honey melon and watermelon. They were just sitting on the kitchen side to be eaten over the weekend.

Walking through the door and saying my hellos, I noticed my brother innocently sat watching TV, no more than 3 metres away. My first thought was "let me throw the melon at him and see if he can catch it". For all those with siblings, this is a completely rational thought. So, I dropped my keys, grabbed the melon and tossed it over at my brother. To his amazement we ended up spending the next 15 minutes playing what we called 'don't drop the melon'. This was the first time I remember real happiness after stopping drinking or at least in a very long time. The event culminated in me throwing the watermelon at my Mum and her blaring out the most over dramatic scream. It was a real belly-laugh moment.

This reconnection with my inner child to form activities and starting to plot a life post alcohol had begun.

A FOUNDATION

Having spoken openly about my previous romantic relationships with Georgie, I had now got a second chance. All the data indicates that individuals who are single drink more alcohol.[4] There are many cultural reasons for this, but one that I have looked into is loneliness. In the HALT acronym, which I shared in Chapter 7, Alone was one of the feelings to avoid. With one exception, across all research groups, ages and stages of life, women frequently report higher levels of loneliness than men. That exception is single people.[5] There are many factors around this: less than half of men report being satisfied with their friendships and only about one in five say they have received emotional support – this is compared to 4 in 10 women.

This is where I was going. There are significant advantages for men to be in stable happy relationships.

Marriage benefits men – and more so than it does women – in numerous different ways. Research[6] shows that happily married men:

§ Are healthier overall.

§ Live longer – in fact, one study[7] showed that having a partner in middle age is protective against premature death.

§ Show improved cancer outcomes.

§ Have better heart health.

§ Are less likely to engage in risky or unlawful behaviour.

§ And even have stronger bones.

I'm not saying that those of other genders or in relationships that fall outside the bracket of marriage can't experience the same outcomes. As this study acknowledges, there
simply isn't the data available to say definitively either way.
However, what this study demonstrates is that certainly
for men, being in a stable, happy relationship makes them
healthier and happier.

This aligns with my own experiences. The happier I
became and the more emotional support I had around me,
the less I wanted to drink alcohol. Being in a strong, stable
relationship was a crucial part of my recovery.

A great relationship provides a constant source of social
connection. A great relationship leads to enduring friendship, which can boost well-being and confidence. Finding
the right relationship was so important for me. I had experienced good relationships before, which ended due to no
fault other than life taking us in different directions.

On the day I stopped drinking, I had been with Georgie
for only 1 month – I believe this was perfect. If it had
been any longer, we may not have been in the honeymoon
exciting stage, and it would have been easier for her to
walk away. At this point, nothing had been formalised
and we had just started something that felt exciting and
new. That meant we could put my behaviour on the day of
the races down to a bad mistake, but a mistake that I had
learned from. Rather than glossing over it and continuing
to date more casually, we could commit to building something – but I had to be committed. My actions had to align
with my words.

When looking at the overall positives of my journey to my rock bottom and being able to recover, I put a lot of this down to fortune and having a partner who loved me despite my flaws and was willing to stand by me. This felt like a real sliding door moment in which two major events happened. Not only did I commit to my relationship with Georgie, but I also committed to changing my life and becoming a better person.

With an ultimatum, you have a choice. I had a choice. The easier decision to make at this point would have been for her to walk away from the relationship and the embarrassment I had caused. I could in essence then wash my hands and put the experience down to another failure. But just as I was willing to run headfirst at and tackle the problems I was having professionally, so I would tackle the problems I was facing personally. I felt there was something forming with this woman, so I took the harder path of staying with her and proving to everyone that I was better than 'Drunk Dom'. That I was someone who she could love, respect, and treasure.

This was the best slice of fortune, because she brought a lot to my life, even in a short space of time.

I WANTED TO FEEL WANTED

At this point in my life, the biggest thing I felt was missing was a loving relationship. There's something beautiful about two people wanting to spend time with one another and be part of each other's lives. I wanted to share my life with somebody, and I wanted someone who felt the same way. I was reasonably healthy (aside from the alcohol), and I had set up a business that was doing incredibly well. But I was really lonely. I'd gone from being at university, where I was living with my friends and always had people around, to living alone and working as an entrepreneur. I'd had to adjust to a new city, as well as a completely new lifestyle.

I Wanted to Find My Best Friend and Biggest Supporter

Everyone views relationships differently, but I've always seen a strong relationship as an opportunity to not only be with your best friend, but also to be with your biggest supporter – and for me to fulfil those roles in return. I wanted to meet someone who I could support and celebrate achievements with – both theirs and mine. I also wanted to make someone else proud of me. I've said it before, but I was incredibly lucky to have Georgie alongside me on my journey as a confidante who I could talk to, and as someone who not only supported me but who continued to do the best for herself. I'm incredibly proud of her and everything she has achieved.

I Needed Affection

I not only needed affection, but also an emotional and physical connection with someone I cared about. I'm sure many people can relate to this. When I hit my rock bottom, I was living in a four-storey house, with seven bedrooms, in the suburbs outside Manchester. Steve and I never even went down to the bottom floor. It felt eerie. The floors were tiled and cold underfoot. It always felt as though something was missing – it was a house but it certainly wasn't a home. There's a certain irony looking back now on that period just before I stopped drinking – there I was in a beautiful house, utterly miserable and drinking alone. The house felt as empty as I did. I needed the warmth, affection and love of a real home, and I wanted to create that sense of home with a partner.

Affection has a positive impact at every stage of our lives. Research shows that people who received high levels of parental affection as babies and young children had higher self-esteem, were more resilient and happier, and were less likely to be anxious and stressed as adults than those who received low levels of affection from their parents.[8]

A GOOD PARTNER IS CONTINUOUSLY ENCOURAGING

Who's the person who cheers you on when you're getting close to achieving a goal or milestone? When I started on my sober journey I needed someone to encourage and support me perhaps more than I ever had before. As a young man in my early 20s, I viewed life very simply in terms of my work, my health, and romantic relationships. The latter was where I felt I had a void.

The truth was that I had no idea what I was doing in my life. Often I was just winging it. I was riddled with self-doubt when I started my sobriety journey. So having someone alongside me on this path who could either help me sense-check my actions or be really encouraging when I was going in the right direction was really important.

I found that support and encouragement in my relationship with Georgie, and I am happier and healthier for it. But this support doesn't come exclusively from romantic relationships. It could just as easily come from friends, family or a business partner, and in my experience having people around who can champion you when you're battling an addiction is incredibly valuable.

I've already mentioned the famous Jim Rohn quote about being the equal of the five people you spend the most time with – given that you probably spend the most time with your life partner, they can have a huge impact on your overall well-being and happiness.

I NEEDED LOVE IN MY LIFE

Being in love made me feel inspired and gave me courage to do what I didn't think I'd be able to. I felt like an imposter in most of my life – I wasn't really a business person or a suit-wearing COO; I was a 22 year old kid who was always in jeans, just trying to figure things out. Looking back, removing myself from my parents and my family was a mistake as it isolated me. It heightened my desire to be loved. At this point in my journey, I wanted to feel accepted and to know that someone could and did love me for who I was.

In my experience, a lot of young men refuse to accept help, even when they really need it. There's a tendency to just get your head down and crack on – I know that's what I did. It's this toxic level of machoism that can make you believe that, as a man, you should be able to shoulder everything and handle the pressure without asking for help. I needed love in my life to help me realise that I didn't have to carry everything alone, and that I could not only ask for help, but have the reassurance that I would receive it.

When I look back at the two months before I stopped drinking, during which time Olivia and I broke up and I started dating Georgie, I'm filled with a sense of gratitude. I didn't realise it when I met Georgie, but she was exactly the person I needed in my life. She was confident, knew what

she wanted and set firm boundaries with me. She told me I
needed to sort myself out. This was different to every other
person I'd dated before – they all went along with the drinking and the partying. I'm not blaming them in any way for
my behaviour, merely pointing out how difficult it is to have
the strength to stand up to someone and tell them "no", to set
those firm boundaries about what you will and won't tolerate.

I receive a lot of messages these days from people's
partners – usually women who are in relationships with
men who have issues with alcohol – asking how to have
that hard conversation. Make no mistake, it's a very hard
conversation to have. If you're in that situation, you have
to make the choice about whether you are going to walk
away from your partner, or stand by them while they tackle
their problems. If you choose to stand by them but you
don't approve of their actions, set out your boundaries, like
Georgie did for me. Doing so might just be the catalyst for
their change. Knowing that someone cares enough about
you to set those boundaries could be what it takes. I know
that helped me. Maybe in your situation things have already
gone too far and you need to walk away. It's not my place to
tell you what to do. I count myself lucky that Georgie had
previously had a relationship with someone who struggled
with alcohol, because that meant when she met me, she was
in a position to set boundaries. She saw enough potential
in me to decide to stick with me – and I'm glad every day
that she did.

Not that I needed reminding of the choices that led to
my sliding door moments on my sobriety journey, but about
a month before Georgie and I got married, I saw Olivia,

the woman I was dating before I met Georgie, for the first time. It was the strangest situation – I was driving and she pulled up alongside me at a set of lights. We clocked each other and nodded, and then she drove off. When I thought back to our relationship, and compared it to what I had with Georgie, I knew I was happier now than I'd ever been. All the actions I'd taken that had pushed Olivia away had led me to the person I believe I'm supposed to be with.

It was also a timely reminder that the risk of temptation is ever-present on your sober journey. Although I talk in the rest of this book about my early experiences of sobriety, there will be moments many years after you've had your last drink that could tempt you to take another sip of booze. For me, seeing Olivia was a reminder of the party lifestyle I used to lead, and that reminder showed me that it wasn't a lifestyle I missed.

BEST LAID PLANS

As I've said, at 23 years old and taking time away from drinking, it was unclear to me what my days, evenings, and weekends would look like without heading to the pub or the nightclub.

At my worst, I would spend well over £150 a week on alcohol alone. This is before adding in hidden costs of drinking – things like taxis and takeaways. Every night out, with Uber on the rise, I would spend £10 here, £10 there on taxis just getting around in a city. This was not including the £30–40 it would cost me to get home. Alongside this, Domino's on a Sunday would be a given, alongside probably another pizza or a kebab on the way home. This sounds like an extreme amount, but it was very real. I am confident in saying that my monthly costs for alcohol (I'm aware that I was not a normal 20-something) would be between £1000–1500 per month.

I was advised to start using an app called Quit for Health. The app gives you a push notification every morning with a note for how many days 'clean' you are. But the genius of this app was a formula that calculated how much money you had saved per week. So every day, based on this formula, I would get a notification saying that I had 'saved' for example £1000 since I last drank. This information was vital. At this point in my life alcohol was my only treat, my only gratification for doing something good. I didn't know how else to celebrate – call this a failure of myself at a younger age – but I hadn't built a positive feedback loop such as the one shown in Figure 8.1.

Not only was my response during negative times in my life to drink, but I found myself drinking during the positive times as well. For example, I remember that deals at work would be in the hundreds of thousands pounds, and when

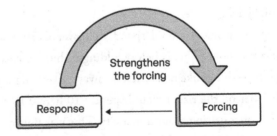

Figure 8.1 Stimulus–response model

these happened, I would sneak off just to grab a beer and toast the success.

I needed a new positive way to react.

The money that I saved from not drinking every week I would make sure I spent on positive, enjoyable occasions. A real treat. This became non-negotiable for me.

At this time in my life, I was spending all my money every month. All the money I saved at this point in my life, I saved by avoiding drinking alcohol. To maintain any change in your life, that change needs to not be viewed as a punishment or restrictive. It needs to be positioned in your mindset as a positive. The reason crash diets don't work is because they are seen as a punishment.[9] If you simply go on a diet and don't permanently change your lifestyle, you will probably gain back the weight. In fact, crash dieting has a dismal long-term success rate of only 5–10%.

The language we use can have a dramatic impact on how we perceive things. A study conducted in the use of language showed participants video clips of car crashes. Later they were asked to estimate the speed of the vehicles when the crash occurred. However, the questions were worded slightly differently. The main question was:

How fast were the cars going when they [blank] each other?

The blank in the question was then replaced with *contacted, hit, bumped, collided,* or *smashed.*

Those who received the question with the word "smashed" estimated the speed much higher than those who received the question with the word "contacted" (see Table 8.1).

Table 8.1 Estimate of speed based on verb
used in question prompt

Verb	Mean estimate of speed (mph)
contacted	31.8
hit	34.0
bumped	38.1
collided	39.3
smashed	40.8

Words and actions, these can make a big difference.
I needed to frame, reinforce, and act in a way that demon-
strated giving up alcohol was a positive decision and that my
life would benefit from this. I knew that doing this at the
start of my journey would increase my chances of success.

So rather than sitting at home on a Friday night, scroll-
ing through stories of all the things I was missing out on, I
needed plans and occasions that would enhance my experience of sobriety rather than make me regret my decisions.

I created three rules that I followed religiously, to make
the most of my life and survive.

§ Write a to-do list

As with journaling at work, I decided to use to-do lists
to tackle the tasks I wanted to do. As I reconnected with my
happy baby, I questioned myself, what do I want to do? This
was a broadening of my own life. So I locked myself away
and I wrote my list of things I really wanted to do.

As part of reconnecting with my happy baby, there was
a list of things I loved that I started to reconnect with. The
first one was football. Growing up I was a big Liverpool fan,
some of my earliest memories were watching Michael Owen
at the 1998 world cup scoring 'that' goal against Argentina.

Many people my age fell in love with football because of that and I was one of them. I had spent every weekend for my entire youth playing football and then I had just stopped.

Spending time on an activity that you enjoy can improve your mental health and well-being. In fact, people with hobbies may be less likely to experience stress, low mood, and depression.[10] I had lost this. Although it had been for only maybe 2 years, the toll it had taken – not doing something I loved – was huge. So I took action – I arranged a weekly five-a-side football match with the team in the office. I did this purposely on a Thursday evening, so that a time I would have normally spent drinking would now be spent on football. I had something in my calendar to avoid falling into old habits like going to the pub. Additionally, I started to go to see Liverpool play. Before giving up alcohol, this always felt like a huge commitment, either having to get a train or a taxi – because there was no point going if I couldn't have a drink. Now I would get a ticket with the money saved from not drinking. I remember buying a ticket and walking into the stadium to watch England vs Scotland at Wembley for the first time, thinking to myself 'not drinking' got me here.

My list also included visiting castles. I wrote a list of ones I wanted to see: Versailles, Edinburgh, and others. My weekends soon became booked up with things I now wanted to do. As my dependency on alcohol increased, I had lost sight of simple things. I kept saying to myself "let's go back to basics" and the to-do list worked.

§ Reward yourself

To build the positive feedback loop, you need to wake up on Monday and be able to say with confidence "I had a great weekend." While your behaviour has changed, those around you haven't. They will still be going out at weekends. You will see it and you can't control them. You can only control yourself.

So, in the WhatsApp chat, the 'water cooler' moment at the office or just to people you meet, you need to be able to say "I did x and it was fantastic." We crave gratification and as a generation our lives are posted online. So being able to have a 'mini win' is important. So with the money saved, I'd buy that new top, I'd upgrade the meal to large – I needed the rewards that weren't alcohol.

§ Remove yourself

Temptation is constantly around us. In the moment, it feels like there is no downside to just having a drink, or going on that night out. Indeed, it has been estimated that up to 40% of deaths in the United States every year are attributable to self-control failures.[11] While my healing and reprogramming hadn't been finalised, I knew I needed to be away from temptation. My plans had to be away from my triggers. It is very easy to blame your social circles as negative influences. I had friends who I had never met sober, who were drinking friends. These were friends you'd make on nights out. People you would gravitate to because you know they liked to drink as well.

All my plans had to be away from these people and in safe environments. Safe environments do not mean being locked in a room with no alcohol around you. That is not a safe environment, it is a mental prison. Clock watching, waiting for evening to come around so you can go to sleep and forget about it – this is not healing. I removed myself from being exposed to dangerous environments and put myself in safer, more positive situations. These are small changes of physically moving yourself or emotionally removing yourself. One of the safest places I found was the cinema. This was at the peak of Netflix and other streaming services revolutionising movies. For me, though, sitting in the cinema with a bag of popcorn, drinking a slushy was safe. It was a meaningful evening keeping myself mentally stimulated.

These rules work well, but I knew there would come a time or a situation when I had to 'go out again'. I was building myself up again for this – with confidence knowing that I wouldn't drink again.

BACK WE GO

I spoke at length with Chris Williamson on the Modern Wisdom podcast[12] about alcohol use. His view is that we use alcohol to sedate ourselves around boring friends or situations we don't want to be in. Drinking is the lubricant that we use in social situations we don't want to be in. Further, his view on addiction was that it isn't until we reintroduce the addiction into our lives that we are truly healed.

This was a point I dwelled on. It was hard to feel that the only way I could be healed, or handle alcohol was to reintroduce it. My viewpoint on this was that it wasn't until I started to move back into my 'normal life' that I would be able to be truly healed.

Avoidance and trying to build a new life was my coping strategy for the first few months, but there was no way for the rest of my life I could avoid birthday parties, weddings, celebrations, or funerals. These are normal parts of life that we all go through and at some point I would have to attend one.

Weddings are some of the biggest occasions we have in our lives. I had my own wedding in July 2023. When I stopped drinking, I held onto being able to toast and celebrate this moment with my wife.

We've all been to weddings where we don't know people and we want to 'break the ice' and fit in with others. I attended a wedding in 2017, sober, and heard the worst drunken horror story of a wedding. One of the guests, who was a plus-1 at the wedding and didn't really know the bride or the groom, was very heavily drunk and accused the groom of sleeping with one of the bridesmaids in the toilet at the wedding breakfast. Now, I can categorically confirm that the groom did not sleep with one of the bridesmaids, but this in itself is an advert for not drinking. For me, I had to build a framework of coping with these situations in the short term, to give me the ability to be around people and not be tempted to drink again.

More and more people are choosing not to drink, so even though it might seem that you're the only person not drinking alcohol in certain situations, like at a wedding, there are far more people on a sober journey than you might think.

Figure 8.2 shows a graph of Google searches about 'stopping drinking'. The interest and demand over time has increased dramatically.

My strategy, when reintroducing myself to nights out, was to continue to be in control and follow the guidelines

Interest over time ⑦   ⬇ ‹› ⦉

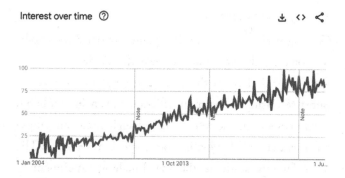

Figure 8.2 Google search frequency on the term 'stop drinking' over time

that Jamie and HALT set me: Never be 'tired, hungry, cold'. There were also many more strategies and principles to follow. I've shared them here and I hope they help you too.

ALWAYS DRIVE

This is the easiest, go-to strategy to have control of your evening or night. We have been bombarded with the admonition 'Do not Drink and Drive' – which people still do not follow. In 2022 in the United States 28 people a day were killed in drunk driving incidents. This equates to roughly one person every 52 minutes.[13] Getting behind the wheel after even having one drink is not worth the risk. Alcohol severely hampers a driver's ability to safely operate a car – slowing reaction time and impairing judgement.

If you want to go to any occasion, having your car there gives you responsibility to get yourself (or others) home safe. The secondary piece is that it also gives you the ability to leave on your terms. You don't have to stay until the end, because truthfully nothing good happens after 2.00 am.

PLAN EARLY MORNING ACTIVITIES

Coming back to the 'to-do list', giving myself responsibilities for early the next morning was the single best way to focus my mindset on the future rather than the present. Short-termism is a common affliction and an ancient habit. Technological developments have heightened our short-term tendencies.[14] This has been widely researched. The most famous study is the marshmallow experiment.[15] The experiment began by bringing each child into a private room, sitting them down in a chair, and placing a marshmallow on the table in front of them.

At this point, the researcher offered a deal to the child: "I'm going to leave the room and if you don't eat the marshmallow while I'm away, you will be rewarded with a second marshmallow. However, if you decide to eat the first one before I get back, you won't get the second one."

So the choice was simple: one treat right now or two treats later.

The researcher left the room for 15 minutes.

I'm sure you can imagine the footage the researchers captured. Some of the kids barely waited for the door to close before they'd eaten the marshmallow. Others held out a little longer, wiggling and bouncing around in their chairs, but still gave into temptation. There were a few children who waited the entire 15 minutes and received their reward of a second marshmallow.

What many people don't know about the study was that there was a follow up. The children who were willing to delay gratification and waited to receive the second marshmallow ended up having higher SAT (standard

assessment test) scores – these are tests taken at the ages
of 7 and 11 in the United Kingdom's education system –
lower levels of substance abuse, lower likelihood of obesity,
better responses to stress, better social skills as reported
by their parents, and generally better scores in a range of
other life measures.

The researchers followed each child for more than
40 years. What's really interesting is that the group who
resisted temptation and waited patiently for the second
marshmallow consistently succeeded in whatever capacity
the researchers were measuring. As the article notes:

*In other words, this series of experiments proved that the ability
to delay gratification was critical for success in life.*

*And if you look around, you'll see this playing out every-
where:*

§ *If you delay the gratification of watching television and get
your homework done now then you'll learn more and get
better grades.*

§ *If you delay the gratification of buying desserts and chips at
the store, then you'll eat more healthily when you get home.*

§ *If you delay the gratification of finishing your workout
early and put in a few more reps then you'll be stronger.*

Or think about taking that single drink on a night
out – having that drink that night is much easier than getting up early to do something else. Delaying and changing
your gratification from that well-earned pint on a Friday
night allows you to do an early morning drive to tick off
something on your 'to do list' like visiting Edinburgh.

Know Your Tribe

Who is around you – what they have got you thinking, saying, doing, and becoming – sets the course of your life. In the words of motivational speaker Jim Rohn: "You are the average of the five people you spend the most time with." The people you spend the most time with shape who you are.

When going on nights out or to weddings, you have to know who your five people are. Who are those that you spend your time with? The brutal honest truth is that you have either friendships or 'situationships' (a relationship that has formed because you are in a similar situation). Take work friends. The honest truth is that these people are not your friends. I've had a number of relationships (platonic and romantic) that have blossomed in specific situations but as soon as that situation changes, for example, someone leaves the office – the relationship dies.

I had many friends that I only really knew through drinking. I had even more friends when I was buying drinks for people. These weren't really friends. I called them my 'drinking buddies', and at the same time I felt like my relationships with my real friends had weakened. The easiest way to understand whether a drinking buddy is a real friend or not, is to tell them, "I am not drinking because it is not good for my health." A real friend will say, "I am here to support you." Someone who doesn't value your friendship but only wants company while they drink will come up with the line similar to, "Don't be boring."

"Don't be boring" is an expression I've heard more times than I can begin to count – I've heard it in relation to drinking, drugs, and even doing crazy stupid stuff, which has the potential to be extremely dangerous or damaging.

Being boring is an innate fear – it stems back to our ancient roots, the fear of being rejected by our tribe, which, in the hunter-gatherer era, would result in death. Not having others around you to support you would be fatal. Preventing being expelled from the tribe depended on getting others to like you; if members of the tribe liked you, then you would not be rejected. That said, our brains evolved to fear rejection because rejection could mean the end of your life. We fear boring because we do not want to face rejection.

What is the cost of trying to 'fit in?' How far will we go to please others to the detriment of our own mental health? There is nothing worth putting ahead of your mental health. There is no night out or alcohol that is worth perceived acceptance.

People evolve and change and the truth of the matter is that people who resonate with you on a deep level aren't always the ones who happen to be born in the same year as you or happen to live in the same location as you or happened to end up in the same university accommodation as you.

Although our shared experiences are valuable, we are all unique individuals formed by our own experience. Holding your hand up and saying, "I need help" and "I need to stop drinking", thereby going against what is deemed normal within your friendship groups, is difficult but the change is worth it.

I was fortunate; my tribe, my people, understood that I needed to make this change in my life and not once did anyone close to me pressure me into drinking. They never excluded me or pushed me into doing something I didn't want to do. But I also found a new tribe, those like me who couldn't, wouldn't, shouldn't drink alcohol. The warmth I received from those who were like me, was like no feeling I had ever experienced. The truth I discovered was that shared experiences matter, but every single person who's gone through the realisation that alcohol doesn't agree with them has similar journeys and you are automatically connected to those who have also struggled with addiction. There are many of us, and the community is growing.

Your tribe will protect you; they will be there for you.

I know that now, if I was ever for any reason tempted to go for a drink, there are a large number of people who would drop what they are doing and come find me to stop me. The fear of rejection I had on Day 1 of telling people I don't want to drink again has turned from my belief that this would lead to rejection from the tribe, to now being a main reason my tribe accepts me.

To give you an example of how much my friends have my back, I was out one Christmas and ordered a Guinness Zero. If you've ever seen one poured, you'll know it looks like the real deal. As the barman handed my pint to me, one of my friends sprinted across the bar, grabbed my arm and said, "Dom, what are you doing?!" I told him it was Guinness Zero, but he wouldn't let me take the pint until he'd got the barman to confirm this for him.

This to me sums up the paradox of drinking in the United Kingdom – many people drink because of social pressures, but when you have the right people around you, this flips to create an environment where you are pressured to *not* drink. While my drinking started due to social pressures, one of the biggest reasons I now don't drink is due to social pressures. I know that these are real friends. My relationships with them are stronger than any of the "friendships" I formed while I was out drinking, and I feel more connected to those around me than I ever have.

PICK YOUR POISON

This is a topic that is controversial amongst the sober community: how do zero alcohol, low alcohol or alternative drinks factor into recovery? In my situation, I didn't touch a substitute in my first months of sobriety. Although potentially dull and a bit basic, I would continuously drink sparkling water. Although not the most exciting choice, knowing what I would be drinking was safe.

Alcohol substitutes aren't a free-for-all, though. Depending on the brewing process, NA beer may contain small amounts of alcohol, which is incompatible with complete abstinence. Alcohol substitutes can also still trigger unwanted drinking behaviour for some people, so staying away from places where alcohol is served or consumed is important for them.

But there is value in the replacement aspect – holding a drink in your hand, like I did with food, tricking your brain into thinking they are having a beer, can help reprogramme your mind. My advice is to pick what you want and stick with it. Drink on your terms but have lots of water and never get to the point where you feel parched.

Reintroducing yourself to society while wanting to remain sober is difficult, but once you get through these first few occasions you will soon realise your power. Sobriety is a strength, never a weakness.

REWIRING YOURSELF

While I was reconnecting with my happy baby, building a solid life foundation, and tackling work-related issues through my work process, I had continued to use food as my new coping mechanism. This had led to me gaining weight. I had ballooned to over 110 kg for the first time in my life. I gained roughly 15 kg between 24 July and Christmas that year. This was a survival method; I knew I needed to do this.

A few months in, my assistant who had first sent me to get therapy in the first instant said to me:

> Dom, you can't just replace alcohol with burgers, that's not healthy either.

I would effectively over-consume burgers, pizzas, any greasy food I could get my hands on. Any day or evening when I had a slight wobble, I would log into one of the take-away apps and indulge in an 'treat' for myself. I would justify the weight increase to myself as a better decision long term.

My response to my assistant was:

> The burgers are easier to beat.

This was an anecdotal conversation where the words you either say or hear can cut through all your emotions. These ones did. It had become noticeable to those around me that my weight had ballooned. I had replaced one addiction for another, at this point I was no better than I had been previously. I made a promise to others that I was going to improve my health.

We use addictions to cope, and the food was helping me cope without alcohol, but in the long term this was not healthy. Instead of drinking myself into an early grave, I would have eaten myself there. I had now reached 110 kg – for a 6' 3" guy, my BMI here would be morbidly obese.

What I found was that at first the food I replaced alcohol with had to be greasy, it had to be a burger, pizza, Chinese takeaway, or something like that. I found out that high-fat, high-calorie food affects the brain in much the same way as cocaine and heroin.[16] Junk food, alcohol, and drugs such as cocaine gradually overload the so-called pleasure centres in the brain. What eventually happens is the pleasure centres crash. Food was having an effect on me very much like cocaine. Ingredients in purified modern food cause people to 'eat unconsciously and unnecessarily'. The neurotransmitter dopamine appears to be responsible for overeating in the studies. Without knowing, food was my medicine for drinking, it was a way to come off one unhealthy addiction by introducing a replacement.

The major differences and why I said "the burgers are easier to beat" is that all food we eat and the act of eating itself releases dopamine.[17] Even though fatty, high-sugar food increases appetite over time – food in general gives you the same feeling. So although I started with unhealthy

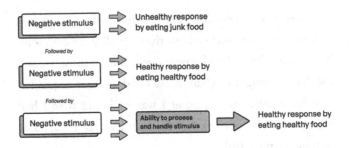

Figure 8.3 Stimulus/response effect on food choices

burgers, chips and so on, the process of replacing this with healthier food was a linear move.

My mental mindset looked like Figure 8.3.

Over the 6 months of recovery, I moved from burgers and pizza to salmon and broccoli as my mental treat to reward my chimp. I slowly moved off the negative food and replaced it with positive food. It wasn't long until I framed in my mind that having salmon and broccoli was my new alcohol, my coping mechanism for dealing with the issues that life was throwing at me.

I'M NEVER DRINKING AGAIN

Coming back to anecdotal conversations that can change your life, there was one that completely convinced me that sobriety was the right and only path for me. My aim when I first stopped drinking was to get 3 months in, and this quickly shifted to 6 months, where I visualised myself celebrating Christmas with a nice glass of red wine.

I frequently brought this up with Jamie as something I wanted to do. I held onto that as a moment that I wanted to experience. All alcohol had an occasion for me.

§ Guinness was to be consumed when the rugby was on or
  I was in an Irish bar.
§ Wine was to be consumed at a nice meal, red with steak
  and white with fish.
§ Rose was to be consumed on a sunny day in Provence.
§ Pimm's was to be consumed at the races in the United
  Kingdom when the weather got up to 22 degrees.
§ Beer was to be drunk at football matches or on a pub crawl
  with friends.

These are stories we are told through advertising, marketing, and content we consume online. This is how the industry operates. They use marketing to create triggers. They are selling experiences to sell products.

Marketing alcohol brands based on occasion is, of course, nothing new.[18] We've long had New Year's Eve, the Super Bowl, St Patrick's Day, 'March Madness', Cinco de Mayo, and the summer US patriotic holidays like Memorial Day and 4 July. What alcohol brands are doing now, however, is identifying occasions that may happen at any time, like birthdays, or the celebration of landing a major new contract at work. As an adjunct to occasion marketing, many of these brands are turning to 'influencers' and occasions headlined by them.

Having a perfectly stocked liquor cabinet isn't really the goal right now, especially with younger consumers. What today's consumers are after is the experience, and when alcohol brands demonstrate they have the products that go perfectly with the experiences consumers want, they market the experience while selling the products, and everyone wins − or everyone thinks they do.

I had managed to break with the majority of the occasions when I normally drank and replaced some with 0.0 alcohol options, but the one I couldn't break was a toast of champagne celebrating a major achievement. This was the last thing I had to break.

There were two conversations I had that removed this thought from my mindset. The first occurred on a night out back in York. It was the festive period, but before Christmas. I bumped into someone I would call an associate. I knew him, but not very well and we would occasionally see each other on nights out. That said, I was always inspired by him and his dedication to fitness. In no creepy way at all, he always had a very impressive physique. He had begun competing in bodybuilding and winning awards. He had something that I was incredibly envious of: the best six-pack you can imagine, always posting pictures online. I used to think to myself – if I had Jack's body, my life would be so different. He would always have women around him. He was someone I looked up to without realising and to this day, he has no idea that what he said one night had an impact on my life.

On a night out, without really thinking he said to me:

Dom, I heard you're doing this sober thing.

To which I replied,

Yeah, I am coming up to 6 months now.

The words he said next have stuck with me ever since. He said, with a JD & Coke in his hands . . .

Man, I could never do what you've done.

He then got pulled away and walked off. Since then I haven't seen him or spoken to him, mainly because my social circles have changed, and I don't go out as much as I used to.

The words struck me and an enlightening moment occurred – it would be the closest thing to an epiphany. For a large amount of my life, I never thought I could do what Jack has done. The guy is a body builder, has the best body, and is one of the coolest guys in my school year. He has just told me, he can't do what I've done. But I knew, there was no way I could do what he'd done.

This occurred at the same place where I met Steven and decided to drop out of university. That conversation with Jack happened about 5 metres away from where those other sliding door moments in my life had taken places. I stood and reflected on this briefly.

Where previously I felt shame in my drinking, now I found celebration in my sobriety. I found myself thinking, *people are proud of me and raising what I am doing on a pedestal of achievement to the point that someone who is incredibly disciplined in their own life couldn't do what I'm doing.* It was in this brief conversation that my entire mentality shifted from

'Me not drinking is something to be ashamed about.'

To

'Me not drinking is something to be proud of.'

The second conversation that changed my position happened the following Monday with Jamie. Meeting with Jamie every Monday made me accountable, I didn't want to walk into his meeting room and tell him, "Hey, last week I had a drink."

I would have felt like I had let him down if I did this. He became my sponsor, my coach, my mentor, and I respected him and felt like he was invested in my journey. So that Monday I came to him to tell him about the experience I had that weekend.

I told him about the interaction I had with Jack and how I felt afterwards. Despite my mindset shift, I still held on to the idea that having a drink at Christmas would be nice to celebrate the achievement, to which Jamie's words of advice were:

If we were talking about cocaine, would you say you'd do a line of cocaine at Christmas to celebrate?

If we were talking about heroin, would you say you'd inject yourself at Christmas to celebrate?

If we were talking about cigarettes would you say you'd smoke at Christmas to celebrate?

The same applies to drinking.

Why would you reward yourself with the poison you consumed as a way of congratulating yourself?

In that moment, the chain of dependency and the emotional relationship I had with alcohol had ended. It had taken almost 6 months of intense therapy, personal development, and desire, but I had gone from the trajectory of being an alcoholic to sober. It was at this moment I first counted myself as sober. I'd travelled the long road of redemption.

NOTES

1. Health Encyclopedia (2023). Journaling for emotional wellness. University of Rochester. https://www.urmc .rochester.edu/encyclopedia/content.aspx?ContentID =4552&ContentTypeID=1#:~:text=Journaling%20 helps%20control%20your%20symptoms,ways%20 to%20better%20control%20them

2. WebMD Editorial Contributors (2012). Mental health benefits of journaling. https://www.webmd.com/ mental-health/mental-health-benefits-of-journaling

3. Margareta Sjöblom, Kerstin Öhrling, and Catrine Kostenius (2018). Useful life lessons for health and well-being: adults' reflections of childhood experiences illuminate the phenomenon of the inner child. *International Journal of Qualitative Studies on Health and Well-being*, 13(1): 1441592. https://www.ncbi.nlm.nih.gov/ pmc/articles/PMC5844049/

4. Robert Prediet (2016). Who drinks more – couples or singles? CBS News. https://www.cbsnews.com/ news/who-drinks-more-couples-or-singles/#:~:text= The%20researchers%20looked%20at%20more, who%20were%20single%20or%20divorced

5. Kira Asatryan (2015). Surprising differences between lonely women and lonely men. PsychCentral. https:// psychcentral.com/blog/surprising-differences- between-lonely-women-and-lonely-men#1

6. Harvard Health Publishing (2019). Marriage and men's health. https://www.health.harvard.edu/mens-health/marriage-and-mens-health

7. Springer Science+Business Media. (2013). 'Marriage linked to better survival in middle age; Study highlights importance of social ties during midlife.' ScienceDaily. 10 January. www.sciencedaily.com/releases/2013/01/130110102342.html

8. Co, P., & Co, P. (2024, February 14). *How a parent's affection shapes a child's happiness for life.* The Gottman Institute. https://www.gottman.com/blog/how-a-parents-affection-shapes-a-childs-happiness-for-life/

9. Lori Rice (n.d.). Why diets don't work. MyFoodDiary .com. https://www.myfooddiary.com/blog/why-diets-dont-work

10. Head to Health (n.d.). Purposeful activity. https://www.headtohealth.gov.au/living-well/purposeful-activity#:~:text=Spending%20time%20on%20an%20activity,feel%20happier%20and%20more%20relaxed

11. Ali H. Mokdad, James S. Marks, Donna F. Stroup, and Julie L Gerberding (2004). Actual causes of death in the United States, 2000. *JAMA* 291(10): 1238–1245. doi:10.1001/jama.291.10.1238.

12. https://www.youtube.com/watch?v=zlYPicjK4U4&t=20s

13. Elizabeth Rivelli (2022). Drunk driving statistics. Bankrate. https://www.bankrate.com/insurance/car/drunk-driving/

14. Ari Wallach (2022). Why is it so hard to escape short-term thinking? Biology and technology. In *Longpath.*

HarperOne. https://bigthink.com/the-present/escape-short-term-thinking/#:~:text=Biology%20and%20technology,How%20can%20we%20fight%20it%3F&text=Short%2Dtermism%20is%20a%20common%20affliction%20and%20an%20ancient%20habit

15. James Clear (n.d.). 40 Years of Stanford Research found that people with this one quality are more likely to succeed. https://jamesclear.com/delayed-gratification

16. Sarah Klein (2022). Fatty foods may cause cocaine-like addiction. Health.com. https://edition.cnn.com/2010/HEALTH/03/28/fatty.foods.brain/index.html

17. Images, G. (2022, December 29). Much of our food is increasingly manufactured to be irresistible to us. Experts say this trend has long-term health consequences. *National Geographic.* https://www.nationalgeographic.co.uk/science-and-technology/2022/12/how-sugar-and-fat-affect-your-brain

18. Greg Keating (2018). How alcohol brands are benefitting from 'occasion' marketing. Hangar12. https://www.hangar-12.com/blog/how-alcohol-brands-are-benefitting-from-occasion-marketing

CHAPTER 9

SUNSHINE IN SOBRIETY

Alcohol is the only drug that you must justify not taking.

Alcohol is a quick fix and with it you find everything you think that alcohol brings you. Alcohol, like other depressants, slows down the central nervous system. This can lead to feelings of relaxation, confidence, and lowered inhibitions.

For the first 6 months, I was treading water, but I was surviving and healing. As I previously mentioned, I couldn't remember the longest time I had gone without drinking. I thought hangovers were a normal part of life. Just something we had to live with by getting a can of coke, a Domino's pizza, and struggling through the day to get it over. This was the norm, or the norm for me. On my journey to remove alcohol from my life, it had taken almost 6 months to rewire my brain to accept that I would not drink alcohol again. The trauma, my issues, my demons, my coping had been dealt with.

During an in-depth conversation with Dr Rangan Chatterjee, author of the book *Happy Mind, Happy Life*, he shared a personal experience of picking up a glass of wine and drinking it for the first time having not had an alcoholic drink for 3 months – he said "instantly I just didn't like what the drink did to me" after a period of time off drinking – in returning to having a glass of wine, it was almost like his body rejected the poison. It is only when you take a break from something you can truly see if you need that in your life or whether your life is richer without it. This is where I had reached, 6 months without and I knew my life was brighter without alcohol in my life.

Many of us have had that feeling of being fresh on a Monday morning after not drinking; the clarity of mind, energy, and a buzz around you. It was scary reading just how long it takes for alcohol to leave your body (see Figure 9.1).

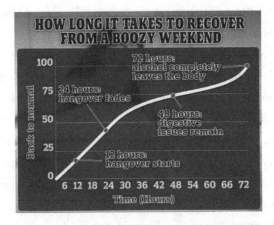

Figure 9.1 How long it takes to recover from drinking
Source: Emily Joshu (2023, 29 November). Expert reveals exactly how long it takes for your body to return to normal after a full weekend of drinking – and it's longer than you think. MailOnline. https://www .dailymail.co.uk/health/article-12797045/body-changes-weekend-drinking-alcohol.html

Figure 9.1 shows that it takes over 72 hours for alcohol to leave the body, meaning those few drinks you might have on a Friday night, just about leave your system by the time you leave the office on a Monday evening.

Though it's common now with Sober October or Dry January to be exposed to the benefits of not drinking for 28 days, you might be surprised just how much it benefits you. The effects of completing one of these 'challenges' include:

§ Better looking skin:

More water is absorbed, premature ageing of skin prevented, skin is hydrated, increase of cell turnover.

§ Liver-function improvement:

Removes contaminants, converts food nutrients, stores minerals and vitamins, regulates blood clotting, helps to fight infections. Liver fat can fall by 15%.

§ Calories saved

Over a 4-week period you can save *up to* 4000 calories by not drinking.

§ Your memory will begin to improve

Alcohol is proven to hinder the part of your brain that deals with memory (the hippocampus).

However, all of these are reversed when you start drinking again and 1 month is not long enough to feel real change and benefit from the true superpowers of sobriety.

One thing I've observed as I've continued my journey to sobriety is that most of us spend our lives looking for 'personal bests'. We look to improve ourselves however we can – whether that's running a marathon, doing a couch to 5k, getting promoted at work, eating more healthily or even reading more books. Just imagine how amazing it would feel if you could wake up every morning as your personal best. That's what sobriety offers.

After reaching 6 months of sobriety, and not having the requirement for alcohol anymore I also began to notice I was able to handle my stress triggers better. My mental capability had increased. There were three main benefits, not talked about as much as others, that I started to experience in sobriety. While areas like improved liver function and cardiovascular health are well known, the following three aren't always as visible.

BETTER SLEEP

We spend approximately one-third of our lives asleep. Sleep is an essential and involuntary process, without which we cannot function effectively.[1] It is as essential to our bodies as eating, drinking, and breathing, and is vital for maintaining good mental and physical health. Sleeping helps to repair and restore our brains, not just our bodies. Alcohol hinders sleep quality. That's because alcohol disrupts what's known as your sleep architecture, the normal phases of deeper and lighter sleep we go through every night. A night of drinking can 'fragment', or interrupt, these patterns, experts say, and you may wake up several times as you ricochet through the usual stages of sleep.[2]

Here's the breakdown: During the first half of the night, when your bloodstream still contains relatively high alcohol levels, you're likely to experience deep, dreamless sleep.

This is due, in part, to alcohol's impact on gamma-aminobutyric acid (GABA) in the brain, a neurotransmitter that calms nerve impulses. Alcohol also inhibits rapid eye movement (REM) sleep, the stage where most dreaming occurs.

Later in the night, as alcohol levels decrease, your brain becomes more active, potentially leading to restlessness. Dr R. Nisha Aurora,[3] a member of the board of directors of the American Academy of Sleep Medicine, noted that as alcohol levels decline, sleep may become more fragmented. This stage may bring about more vivid or stressful dreams, and since disrupted sleep leads to more frequent awakenings, you're more likely to remember these dreams.

Alcohol acts as a diuretic, increasing urine output and potentially causing you to wake up to use the bathroom. Dr Bhanu Prakash Kolla,[4] an associate professor of psychiatry at the Center for Sleep Medicine at the Mayo Clinic, mentioned that moderate amounts of alcohol, particularly wine and spirits, have an early diuretic effect, especially in older individuals. It's unclear whether the urge to urinate is what wakes you up, or if you're simply more attuned to your body during the second half of the night due to fitful sleep.

Alcohol consumption can also lead to increased snoring. It acts as a muscle relaxant, which relaxes the muscles in your upper airways, potentially causing disrupted breathing. For people with obstructive sleep apnoea, who already experience airway collapse during the night, drinking can be particularly risky.

Most experts agree that alcohol negatively affects sleep, regardless of your age or gender. Due to alcohol's depressant effects on the central nervous system, experts advise against combining it with sleep aids like Ambien, Tylenol PM, Benadryl, or supplements such as melatonin. Dr Ilene M. Rosen,[5] a sleep medicine doctor at the University of Pennsylvania, emphasised that alcohol is a sedative and recommended avoiding any sedative – hypnotic substances when drinking.

But what difference does having better sleep have?

Having good sleep literally makes you live longer. Among men and women who reported having all five quality sleep measures (a score of five), life expectancy was 4.7 years greater for men and 2.4 years greater for women compared to those who had none or only one of the five favourable elements of low-risk sleep.[6]

As a man, if I wanted to live almost 5 years longer – is sleeping longer all I need to do? What a life hack that is. When previously I was running on empty – some days having only 4 to 5 hours of sleep and 'burning the candle at both ends' – I often found myself almost oversleeping. In the first months of stopping drinking, however, I was getting close to having 9 hours a day on average. My body would become tired around 9.00 or 10.00 pm and I'd sleep through all the way to 7.30/8.00 am.

This soon became my life hack. There was a major knock-on impact in the rest of my life – I found myself having more energy to attack the day. This energy led to me being able to tackle my increased weight. After the first 6 months, I caught the running bug and did the unthinkable, I signed up for the London Marathon. This was off the back of me finding myself coming home after work at

10.00 pm at night and having the excess energy to go for a run. I would be doing 10 km in the depths of winter in the middle of the night. In these moments there were no limits to what I felt was possible. All because of better sleep, I found myself losing 20 kg in the next 6 months.

Mood

Alcohol is a plaster for your mood, in the short term it increases dopamine and serotonin – the two happy hormones. Addictive drugs can provide a shortcut to the brain's reward system by flooding the nucleus accumbens with dopamine. Additionally, addictive drugs can release 2 to 10 times the amount of dopamine that natural rewards do, and they do it more quickly and reliably.[7] Long term, it depletes them; a short-term hit with long-term sacrifices.

Sobriety is the other way round, short term, you experience a bit of self-consciousness, in a sense you feel slightly insecure and out of place, in environments where you used to thrive. You internalise things and become a stranger in your own mind. The brain can recover but it does take real time. After 1 month of abstinence, the brain looks quite different than a healthy brain; however, after 14 months of abstinence, the dopamine transporter levels (DAT) in the reward region of the brain (an indicator of dopamine system function) return to nearly normal function.[8]

A good friend once said to me, every cell in your body has been developed by what you consume into your body. On average, the cells in your body are replaced every 7 to 10 years. But those numbers hide a huge variability in lifespan across the different organs of the body. Neutrophil cells (a type of white blood cell) might only last 2 days, while the cells in the middle of your eye lenses will last your entire life.[9] This also includes your brain, the computer of your body, which is responsible for every autonomous thought or action. So there are no surprises that after heavy consumption of drugs or alcohol there is going to be damage to the brain.

What I found was that I developed what I called a 'mono mood'. A single constant mood. I could have had the worst day of my life, everything would have been a major crisis or, as we called it in business, a 'fire'. Learning from the stimulus model, the stimuli were always going to occur and in fact, they actually became more aggressive and serious to deal with.

Previously, I would react and respond to these and become heightened, threatened. When we feel danger or threatened we enter the flight or fight mode, with cortisol activated – there are a number of coping methods that I applied. Thanks to my Quaker background, in which we'd sit in silence in our daily meeting, I would find myself in a quiet state processing and recovering. With this, the key was also not to get too excited. These occasions in work would include several issues, like legal issues, tax and cash-flow matters. But as I was running a company with over 200 people, these moments were getting worse and becoming more stressful. Having my mono mood meant that I was able to handle myself in all situations. This became a professional expertise; being calm and able to react positively to a situation with a level head. No longer were my moods up and down. Developing a 'mono mood' in sobriety has expanded my career and businesses beyond where even I saw my potential.

CONFIDENCE

Dutch courage – I have mentioned earlier in this book how we search for it at the bottom of a bottle. It's that liquid confidence to be able to go and talk to someone new we find attractive across the bar, to be able to handle awkward, new social situations. We all crave confidence. I won't forget being in the VIP area of a very exclusive bar in New York, a few months after stopping drinking. I was back in the place where I had my last exciting night out, where I felt confident and happy. I walked into the VIP area, everyone had bottles of champagne, the sparklers were out and the night was 'popping'. I walked up to the bar and ordered a cup of tea.

I won't forget the look on the face of the waitress, thinking to herself, "what the hell is he doing?". She checked with her manager that they could serve me a cup of tea in the club. They could.

I then walked through the VIP area with my pot of tea, saucers and tea cup. I will never forget people coming up to me and stoking conversation. I could have been standing there naked and I would have gotten the same amount of attention. People were shocked. But it went towards me building up my own self-confidence. I felt that I could handle myself in any environment. Confidence is built.

My confidence continued to be built by my improvement in my physical appearance. My improved sleep and healthy eating, all of this added up to a self-perpetuating, positive cycle of healthy choices. And guess what happened when I started sleeping better, eating better, and moving more? My appearance improved. My skin became clear and healthy looking. The puffiness under my eyes decreased.

And although I never guarantee to people that they will lose weight when they quit drinking, and I don't think it should be anyone's primary reason for quitting, dropping a pound or two is usually just a natural consequence of eating better and moving more. (It was for me.) I walked taller and straighter. I became more confident in my appearance.

I remember asking people how old I looked – at 23 I would frequently be told I looked 30. This at first, I thought was a complement. At 18 we desire to look older and be seen to be an adult. I held this with pride. A year after quitting drinking, people would more frequently get my age correct. I looked significantly younger and people saw it.

Sobriety makes you smarter and more interesting. It's quite surprising, but in the past, I genuinely believed that alcohol made me smarter. I thought it had this almost magical ability to supercharge my brain, enabling me to engage in deep conversations on a wide range of topics and make innovative connections between seemingly unrelated ideas.

In hindsight, it's clear that this belief was far from the truth. What I mistook for heightened intelligence was simply the well-known overconfidence that often accompanies alcohol consumption. Looking back, I can't help but think that during those times, I must have sounded rather nonsensical and irrational to those around me. Repeating the same facts over and over again. Sobriety can help make you smarter and keep you smart. Smartness is something to feel confident about.

Quitting itself is an act of courage. Going against culture isn't easy. One of my favourite quotes from J. K. Rowling's work: "It takes a great deal of bravery to stand up to our enemies, but just as much to stand up to our friends."[10] With sobriety we must stand up to our friends and our routines. We have to avoid friends and occasions and change them.

Finally, quitting drinking is an act of self-care, self-love, and self-value. I quit because I care about myself. If you ask yourself why you are considering quitting, you will probably find the same: you want to be sober because you care about yourself too; you care about your appearance; you care about your relationships; you care about making the most of your time; you care about your career; you care about your life; and you love and value yourself.

Through all this, I had built up a new level of confidence that I didn't know was possible. That I didn't believe could exist without drinking.

In truth, everything I thought that alcohol gave me, short term, I found in my sobriety long term. I found the confidence, love, enrichment of my life that I had been seeking, all by removing the drug that I was using to try to find them.

My life started to look more positive, and everything that came after my sobriety was because I didn't drink. I have two major days I celebrate in my life: first, my birthday, I celebrate this like anyone else would; the second more important day is my 'Soberversity', the day I became sober. Every year on 24 July, I take a moment to look back at how far I have come. This day has become bigger than my birthday, it was the day I gave myself the second chance; a second go at everything I loved.

I revisited the list of sober celebrities and their views on sobriety and what it meant to them while writing this book.

Jamie Lee Curtis:[11] "My sobriety has been the key to freedom, the freedom to be me, to not be looking in the mirror in the reflection and trying to see somebody else."

Tom Holland:[12] "I was really, really struggling and I started to really worry that maybe I had an alcohol problem. So I decided that I would wait until my birthday, which is 1 June. I said to myself, 'If I can do six months without alcohol, then I can prove to myself that I don't have a problem.' And by the time I got to June 1, I was the happiest I've ever been in my life."

"It's honestly been the best thing I've ever done, I'm a year-and-a-half into it now. It doesn't even cross my mind. I've found amazing replacements that I think are fantastic, ones that are also really healthy."

Eminem:[13] "I remember when I first got sober and all the shit was out of my system, I remember just being, like, really happy and everything was f**king new to me again."

Gerard Butler:[14] "Maybe a stronger person wouldn't have needed to go (to rehab). When you hear the word rehab, you think, 'He's a mess, he's fucked up.' But I'm glad I did it. I've made a shitload of wrong decisions in my life. But I know I've made some right ones as well."

I searched for someone speaking negatively about their sobriety, I wasn't surprised to find that there wasn't one. When meeting people for the first time, the question I would be faced with, after saying I don't drink, would always be "Why don't you drink?"

My answers have evolved over the years. At first I would avoid and dodge the questions, I would place extrinsic reasoning for it, even going to the extent of saying that

I was just taking a break. There was still an urge in me to fit in and not to alienate people. In truth I was continuing to not be honest, with myself and others – which is how I got into a mess in the first instance. After my first year of being sober and celebrating my first Soberversity, I posted on the social media site LinkedIn, that I was going to be honest:

Today I am 365 Days Sober

1 year ago today I made the difficult decision to stop drinking alcohol.

At the age off [of] 23 this felt scary – I didn't know what my life would look like.

In the past 12 months, I have found so much peace, love, belief in myself and I know it's the best decision I have ever made in my life.

Over these last 12 months, people have asked me 'why did I stop drinking' and the truth is, I have made up countless white lies about the reason why.

The truth is that drinking wasn't good for my mental health, it stole joy and happiness from my life.

From now on I am going to be honest and truthful about the reasons why I stopped drinking – starting with this post.

Thank you everyone for the love and support I have received.

This was the first time I had publicly shared on social media that I had made this decision, the fear I had when I held my finger over the 'post' button was almost overwhelming. The feeling of fear was flushed from me after I quickly saw the outpouring of love and support from people I have never met or hadn't spoken to in years.

One thing you can never escape is the questioning from people you meet. To this day, there hasn't been a social occasion where I haven't been questioned about why I don't drink. This is something that has always fascinated me. As I mentioned, if I had just spent the past year recovering from a cocaine addiction that had ruined my life – would the first thing someone ask me be why I don't do cocaine?

I have explored some of the social reasons alcohol has developed this 'protected status' in society. It is ingrained in our culture, certainly in the United Kingdom and I believe generally across the Western world, but I think the real reason – after talking to hundreds of other people who have taken the sobriety journey alongside myself – is that other individuals are intimidated by the fact that some individuals do not need to drink. They do not need to drink to have fun, to improve their personality, to make them interesting.

Culture and society in the United Kingdom have created the sense that alcohol makes you more fun and life is better with a drink, so the wave of individuals proving that they can handle the same nights out, festivals, weddings, and birthdays without having to drink become intimidating to those that see alcohol as their social lubricator.

This has convinced me that there is no problem in not drinking. But people have a problem with *you* not drinking because of how it reflects on them. This is why I believe it's not uncommon that I'm asked why I don't drink.

Since that first year, my answer has evolved, as I've mentioned. When people first asked me, I went into myself and on the defensive. I slithered out of the question any way possible. After the first year I grew my confidence to give the real reason why I don't drink. Now, my response is simple:

Why do you drink?

Every time, without fail, I receive a look of confusion. This is more than likely a question the person in front of me has never been asked and has no answer for.

There are several common replies that I am faced with, the first one is silence. The second one is defending the volumes of alcohol they drink with a common angle that they are cutting down or recently completed Dry January and Sober October. This question leads everyone to self-reflect.

Why do I drink?

What are the reasons I actually choose to ingest poison directly into my system; again, this is something that remains unanswerable.

As these conversations move forward, I always end them in the same way. I say I will drink again one day, if someone, anyone, (and for people reading this book – this includes you) can give me a genuine reason why I should.

Today, over 7 years in, I haven't had one single drink, but there are many meaningful, real, incredible reasons why you should change your relationship with alcohol.

NOTES

1. *Sleep and mental health* (n.d.). Mental Health Foundation. https://www.mentalhealth.org.uk/explore-mental-health/a-z-topics/sleep-and-mental-health

2. Amelia Nierenberg (2022). Why does alcohol mess with my sleep? *The New York Times.* https://www.nytimes.com/2022/01/25/well/mind/alcohol-drinking-sleep.html#:~:text=That's%20because%20alcohol%20disrupts%20what's,the%20usual%20stages%20of%20sleep

3. Amelia Nierenberg (2022). Why does alcohol mess with my sleep? *The New York Times.* https://www.nytimes.com/2022/01/25/well/mind/alcohol-drinking-sleep.html#:~:text=That's%20because%20alcohol%20disrupts%20what's,the%20usual%20stages%20of%20sleep

4. Amelia Nierenberg (2022). Why does alcohol mess with my sleep? *The New York Times.* https://www.nytimes.com/2022/01/25/well/mind/alcohol-drinking-sleep.html#:~:text=That's%20because%20alcohol%20disrupts%20what's,the%20usual%20stages%20of%20sleep

5. Sleep Myths: Fact or Fiction with Dr Ilene Rosen (n.d.). https://www.youtube.com/watch?v=VGxURe58SO8

6. Nicole Napoli (2023). Getting good sleep could add years to your life. American College of Cardiology. https://www.acc.org/About-ACC/Press-Releases/2023/02/22/21/35/Getting-Good-Sleep-Could-

Add-Years-to-Your-Life#:~:text=Among%20men%20 and%20women%20who,elements%20of%20low%2 Drisk%20sleep

7. Editorial Staff (2024, February 7). *Chemical imbalance & drug abuse in the brain*. American Addiction Centers. https://americanaddictioncenters.org/health-complications-addiction/chemical-imbalance

8. Nora D. Volkow, Linda Chang, Gene-Jack Wang, Joanna S. Fowler, Dinko Franceschi, Mark Sedler, Samuel J. Gatley, Eric Miller, Robert Hitzemann, Yu-Shin Ding, and Jean Logan (2001). Loss of dopamine transporters in methamphetamine abusers recovers with protracted abstinence. *Journal of Neuroscience* 21(23): 9414–9418. https://www.jneurosci.org/content/21/23/9414.full

9. BBC Science Focus (n.d.). What cells in the human body live the longest? https://www.sciencefocus.com/the-human-body/what-cells-in-the-human-body-live-the-longest

10. Rowling J.K. (1997. *Harry Potter and the Philosopher's Stone*. Bloomsbury.

11. Ingrid Vasquez (2023). Jamie Lee Curtis Says she'd 'be dead' without sobriety journey: 'my gratitude is enormous'. *People*. https://people.com/jamie-lee-curtis-speaks-out-about-sobriety-journey-my-gratitude-is-enormous-7567306

12. Zachary Pottle (2023). Tom Holland opens up about sobriety. Addiction Center. https://www.addictioncenter.com/news/2023/07/tom-holland-sobriety/

13. Emily Kirkpatrick (2022). Eminem opens up about getting sober over a decade after his near-fatal drug overdose. *Vanity Fair.* https://www.vanityfair.com/style/2022/09/eminem-sobriety-drug-overdose-2007-relapse-album-paul-pod-podcast

14. Zach Johnson (2012). Gerard Butler finally opens up about rehab. US Weekly. https://www.usmagazine.com/celebrity-news/news/gerard-butler-finally-opens-up-about-rehab-i-havent-had-a-drink-in-15-years-20121910/

FINAL THOUGHTS

The landscape around sobriety has changed significantly in the last 10 years. The conversation has opened up and my hope is that, if you've read this far in the book, you are now more aware that there are many others in the sobriety space who are openly talking about their sobriety journeys, sharing content to help you follow your own sobriety journey if that's what you'd like to do and helping to demonstrate the positive impact that choosing sobriety can have.

One of the beauties of social media is that it allows you to connect with people all over the world. You can build meaningful relationships with likeminded people anywhere in the world, not just in your home city or town. You can find your tribe online, and in my experience what you'll find in the sober community is a welcoming and supportive group of people who want to build each other up however they can.

I've shared my story so openly in this book because I want to open up the conversation about sobriety for more people. Perhaps as you've been reading you've seen yourself in some of the stories I've shared. If you have, then take that as an invitation to reflect on the journey you're on, and where you'd like to go next.

When I was 21, I saw myself as a pretty normal guy. I never expected what would happen in my life over the next 2 years and I definitely wasn't ready for it. My life changed rapidly in a positive way, with the growth of the business, but that positivity very quickly became negative. When I stood at the top of my slope, in September 2015, I could never have imagined how the next 9 months would play out.

On that trip to New York, which I shared in Chapter 1, I felt like I was on top of the world. It never occurred to me at that moment that, just 9 months later, I would literally be at rock bottom having slid down the slipperiest of slopes. My point is, when life throws so much at you so quickly, you can go from having the most incredible moment of your life to having the worst in a relatively short space of time. Life can be great, and life can be difficult. Sometimes it can be great one day and difficult the next.

But just like I had no idea what my life would look like 9 months on from that trip to New York, equally when I was at my lowest I would never have told you that I'd be where I am today, as I write this book – happier and healthier than I've ever been before.

My hope is that reading my story will help you if you're struggling to speak about the challenges you're facing in your life with someone else. I've laid out just how destructive it was for me personally to keep my feelings and struggles bottled up. If you are struggling at the moment, know that there are people who will listen and support you, but you have to take the first step and start that conversation.

I wrote this book because I want to get more people talking, whether that's to their best friend, their parents, their siblings, or a complete stranger online who might be able to help with what they're going through. If this book has helped you in any way, or you would like to know more about me or the journey I've been on, please feel free to reach out via my Instagram: @dpjmcgregor

INDEX